Just Add Actors

Ready-to-serve short plays

Andrew Wetmore

© 2021 Andrew Wetmore

All rights reserved. No part of this book may be reproduced or transmitted in any form or by any means, electronic or mechanical, including photocopying, or by any information storage or retrieval system, without permission in writing from the publisher.

Cover image: A performance of "An Opening" at The King's Theatre, Annapolis Royal, Nova Scotia, as part of the annual King's Shorts Festival of One-Act Plays.

ISBN: 978-1-990187-25-4
First edition November, 2021

MOOSE HOUSE
PUBLICATIONS

2475 Perotte Road
Annapolis County, NS
B0S 1A0

moosehousepress.com
info@moosehousepress.com

We live and work in Mi'kma'ki, the ancestral and unceded territory of the Mi'kmaw people. This territory is covered by the "Treaties of Peace and Friendship" which Mi'kmaw and Wolastoqiyik (Maliseet) people first signed with the British Crown in 1725. The treaties did not deal with surrender of lands and resources but in fact recognized Mi'kmaw and Wolastoqiyik (Maliseet) title and established the rules for what was to be an ongoing relationship between nations. We are all Treaty people.

Performance rights

The copyright for the plays in this book belongs to the author. In buying this book you get the enjoyment of putting on the plays in the theatre inside your head, as you read them.

If you want to perform these scripts in any way, including as a staged reading for a non-paying audience, as an audio play, or as an amateur or professional live or recorded production, you **must** obtain permission in writing from the author. To do otherwise is a violation of copyright and not a nice thing to do to another theatre person.

For information about royalties and obtaining performance rights, send an email to **info@moosehousepress.com**. We will forward serious inquiries to the author.

About these plays

I wrote these plays because an idea struck me, or a path gleamed ahead on my writing pad, and I wanted to find out where it would lead. I did not have a clear idea how any of them would end when I started the first draft.

Fortunately, my characters generally begin to have opinions by the end of the first page. They help me find a way to a script that not only has an ending that makes sense, but that has a body that actors will enjoy performing.

For many years I was artistic director of a theatre company that did a lot of touring. Everything had to fit into the back of one or two vehicles, including the lighting system (we performed a lot in community and parish halls which did not reliably have useful lights aimed at whatever part of the room they called the stage). So I have tended to write "light", with less exploration of special effects and more reliance on the text and how the actors deliver it. "Big Wheel", for example, takes place on a Ferris wheel—but I think it would actually diminish the effect of the play and distract from the text and the characters if you actually created a Ferris wheel and stuck it on your stage.

What the audience can create in their imagination, given just a few clues, is generally more vivid than anything I could write or the stage crew could construct. Performances of "An Opening" and "Customer Service" generally work better if you allude the paintings (in the former) and the posters and toys (in the latter), rather than having them present in painstaking detail.

It is hard to go deep into human emotions or complex questions in a short play, but one can leave pointers, hints, teases... "One-Minute Warning" and "Consequences" have comic touches over an uneasy ground. "Customer Service" is not a play for all age groups.

Here are ingredients that theatre folks can whip up into performances that I believe both they and their audiences will enjoy. They also respond well if you are reading this just for yourself, with all the resources of the theatre of your inner mind available.

Andrew Wetmore
Clementsport, Nova Scotia
October, 2021

~

"At the End of My Rope" first appeared in print in *The Seven Deadly Sins,* a collection of plays by several authors published by Ghostlight Theater Publications of New Hampshire.

"The Story Of" and "Fig" are part of my collection *Fast of Fools,* 18 plays for Christian faith communities to use during the season of Lent.

For my late dad, Stuart Wetmore, whose theatrical career was cut short in the 1940s when his boss, the Anglican Bishop of Fredericton, told him it was inappropriate for a young clergyman to portray Jonathan, the murderous brother, even in an *amateur* production of *Arsenic and Old Lace*.

I have a folder with the unfinished text of a play he was writing for years and years. I hope to finish it for him one day.

The author has created the characters, conversations, interactions, and events of these plays, and any resemblance of any character to any real person is coincidental.

Contents

Performance rights..3
About these plays..5
Ten-minute plays..10
Plays by cast size..11
Poseur..13
An Opening..31
Compliments of the House..49
One-Minute Warning..65
Quiet Car..83
Fig..99
Public Humiliation..111
At the End of My Rope..129
The Face Chords..143
Consequences..157
Customer Service..173
The Story Of..193
Big Wheel..213
An Earthly Nurse..241
Acknowledgements..269
About the author..271

Andrew Wetmore

Ten-minute plays

The plays listed below *probably* fit within the time requirements for ten-minute play festivals. Many have had productions in such festivals or competitions.

Double-check both the event rules and your actual run-time for a given script (reading all the lines and going through all the actions) to make sure. You may not make cuts or other changes to the script without explicit written permission from the author.

Poseur
An opening
Compliments of the House
One-Minute Warning
Quiet Car
Fig
Public Humiliation
At the End of My Rope
Consequences
Customer Service
The Face Chords

Just Add Actors

Plays by cast size

A lot of the scripts specify parts for men and women. Depending on the script, and as long as you do not violate the intention of the play (that is, none of these are spoofs or pantomime scripts, and in several scripts there is a definite sexual attraction or tension between characters), you may opt to fill parts with actors of any gender for most of these plays.

For two actors
Poseur
An Opening
Quiet Car
Fig
At the End of My Rope
An Earthly Nurse

For three actors
One-Minute Warning
Consequences
Public Humiliation

For four actors
Compliments of the House
Customer Service
The Face Chords

For five actors
The Story Of
Big Wheel

Andrew Wetmore

Poseur

Time
Now.

Setting
A room in a former warehouse, now a warren of art studios

Cast

Nell: A writer

Len: An artist's model

Andrew Wetmore

Poseur

A room. A few chairs, with a neat pile of clothing on one chair.

NELL sits with a notebook in her lap; she writes a couple of words on the current page, stares at them. Crosses one out.

LEN ENTERS wearing a short white robe and flip-flops. He does not see Nell. He rotates his arms, stretches.

LEN
Hell of a way to make a living...

NELL
What?

LEN
What?

He sees Nell.

LEN
Oh. What are you doing in here?

NELL
What do you mean?

LEN
You don't oughta be in here.

NELL
Are you the king of the room?

LEN
What?

NELL
This is a free room. I come here all the time.

LEN
Well, you don't oughta be in it when I'm in it.

NELL
Why?

LEN
This is the break room for me. I get to come in here to not be seen, not be on view. Get it?

NELL
Me, too.

LEN
Why aren't you in the other room, where you belong?

NELL
I belong here.

LEN
Then where do I belong?

NELL
Big question for a guy in flip-flops.

LEN
In flip-flops, yes. Yes. And those over there is my sneakers. Under my stuff. In this room.

NELL
That makes it your room?

LEN
How you think my sneakers got there? I was in them when they arrived. In here. And you weren't.

NELL
In your sneakers?

LEN
In my nothing. I was. you wasn't. Get your own room.

NELL
Or you'll do what? Squirt me with sunblock?

LEN
I'm not sunbathing! Where would I sunbathe around here?

NELL
Someplace where I'm not, I hope.

LEN
What's wrong with sunbathing?

NELL
I wouldn't know.

LEN
Yeah, you wouldn't know because you never do it. Am I right?

NELL
I do it.

LEN
But only on a beach where nobody ever ever comes. At night. Just

you and the sand fleas.

NELL
I'm not leaving.

LEN
Who cares what you do?

NELL
You do.

LEN
This is my break room! Excuse me while I take my break.

NELL
From what?

LEN
From the class.

NELL
There's a class?

LEN
I just said. It meets this time every week, I think.

NELL
Look, uh...

LEN
Len.

NELL
Look, Len. There a jillion artists who use this building. A jillion tortured souls exploring their creativity. I have a hard enough time keeping up with myself, much less knowing are there any classes.

LEN
Well, there is.

NELL
Goody. In what?

LEN
In there. That other room.

NELL
No: in what is the class? What is it about?

LEN
It's the life drawing class. So it's about life, which I guess you are not all that familiar with.

NELL
You're the...subject?

LEN
No, this is my painting smock.

NELL
You just stand there. And they look at you. With no flip-flops.

LEN
Which is why I get a break room.

NELL
And then you go back in.

LEN
Three-hour class, not counting the breaks.

Andrew Wetmore

NELL
So you'll be gone soon. Good.

LEN
That's it?

NELL
Carry on with your break.

LEN
All right. I will.

> *Nell ostentatiously concentrates on her notebook. Len watches her; looks around. Moves to a chair. Drags it across the floor experimentally.*

NELL
What are you—?

LEN
My break: I do it my way.

> *Nell looks back down at her notebook. Writes a word. Crosses it out. Len slides his chair and farts at the same time.*
>   *It is a loud fart.*

NELL
What—!

LEN
Sorry.

> *He fans the air.*

NELL
Was that a—oh!

She fans at the air, backs away.

LEN
I said sorry.

NELL
What did you have for breakfast?

LEN
Normal stuff. Guy stuff.

NELL
Do these windows open?

LEN
It'll be okay soon. It sort of settles to floor level.

NELL
Ew.

LEN
Look, when I work a life-drawing class, I have to try to put everything on hold. No runny nose. No grumbly stomach. No—

NELL
For how long?

LEN
Some of the poses are a half hour.

NELL
Oh. That's a hard job.

A thought occurs to her.

NELL
What if—? What if, while you're standing there, lying there...?

LEN
What?

NELL
Nothing.

LEN
That's the first thing people always say.

NELL
Do you just...think of sad things?

LEN
Who wants to think of sad things while they're getting turned on? I don't want that connection in my head.

NELL
I mean to stop it.

LEN
It's got a mind of its own. It wants up, it goes up. Some funny bunny says, 'Hey, this isn't a gesture drawing!' and then everybody feels they got a license to look.

NELL
It must be hard.
(embarrassed)
I mean—

LEN
That's the second thing people say. No, the tough part is, people are sitting all around you. No matter how you pose, some poor sweet soul gets twenty minutes looking at your not-best side.

NELL
What's your not-best side?

LEN
When my break's over you can figure it out.

NELL
I'm not in the class.

LEN
Then what are you doing here?

NELL
I have to be somewhere.

LEN
C'mon: don't lose your nerve now. Bring your sketchbook into the room with the naked guy.

NELL
It's not a sketchbook. I don't sketch. I write. Well...I don't write.

LEN
This is an artist building.

NELL
Writing is art! Can be art.

LEN
But you don't write.

NELL
I try. I put words on the page. But it's not writing, it's just words.

LEN
Keep trying: it'll get better.

NELL
It doesn't get better! My editor keeps talking at me and I can't concentrate. I can't make a single sentence my editor is happy to see. So I try different rooms, different tools. Maybe my editor won't notice if I sit in the parking lot with my laptop, or in here with my notebook for grocery lists. But my editor notices.

LEN
We gotta stop this guy.

NELL
What?

LEN
You can't just run away. We gotta stop him.

NELL
He'll keep coming back.

LEN
You want me to give him the message?

NELL
What?

LEN
I'm pretty fit: you may have noticed. If I encourage him to leave you alone—

NELL
But I need him! I will need him. If I ever write something right through, finish the first draft...I'll need the editor to help me fix it up.

LEN
I see.

NELL
You do?

LEN
You are in what they call an abusitive, abusturbatory relationship. He hurts you, and you keep coming back to him because maybe you think nobody else will have you.

NELL
No. He helps me see things in my writing, problems that I can't see myself. But I can't make him just shut up until I'm done with the first draft.

LEN
He's messing with your head. Dammit, he wants you to fail. Fire him.

NELL
You don't understand.

LEN
Do you?

NELL
It's complicated.

LEN
That's the fourth thing they say.

NELL
What?

LEN
In the drawing class. When I look at what they drew and it isn't me, it's like a ball of yarn the cat got at. "It's complicated."

NELL
What's the third thing they say?

LEN
Oh, that. When their work is going well, and maybe they like the look of you not just as a model, you know? And they want to express their appreciation, they say, 'Your skin takes the light well.'

NELL
'Your skin takes the light well.'

LEN
It's the only safe compliment you can make to the naked model. And you keep eye contact while you're saying it.

He moves close to her.

LEN
Your skin takes the light well.

NELL
Wow. Thanks.

They stare into each other's eyes.

LEN
That was...just like an example, of course.

NELL
Of course.

LEN
Look, my break is almost over.

NELL
You should go.

LEN
But look—

> *He reaches under his robe. She flinches back, hands over her face.*

NELL
No! Not yet! I'm not ready!

LEN
It's a business card.

> *He brings it out. Offers it to her.*

LEN
My business card.

NELL
(taking it)
Okay.

LEN
I don't even know your name.

NELL
Nell.

LEN
Huh. Nell and Len.

NELL
We were...meant to be back to back?

LEN
Yeah, sure. But look: when this editor gets on your case, when it's not his time, just call. Okay?

NELL
Do you get another break?

LEN
Yeah. Maybe. Will you be here still, if I do?

NELL
Yeah. Maybe.

LEN
Then I'll see you sooner than what I thought, Nell.

He crosses to the door.

NELL
Len? Your robe takes the light well.

LEN
That's good. Very good. Write that down. Later.

He EXITS.

NELL
Later.

She grabs her pad and pen, starts to write.

NELL
"His skin took the light well, glinting with that

Mediterranean golden glow that may not actually exist among mere mortals..."

She looks at the text.

NELL
"among mortals...among mere mortals...among mortals--"

She shouts at her inner editor.

NELL
Shut up shut up shut up! It's not your time! We'll fix it when the first draft is DONE!

Pause. She cocks her head. The editor is silent.

NELL
Huh.

She starts to write rapidly.

NELL
"His name was Len and, although his body was toned and a pleasure to look on, he deserved a better life, a life where it was also a pleasure to touch. He did not believe he deserved a better life, and she understood it was going to be her task to teach him."

END

Andrew Wetmore

An Opening

Time
Now.

Setting
An art gallery. A food table to one side. Many paintings by one artist are on display.
　Some productions have dressed the stage with actual paintings in frames, as on the front cover. Others have used empty frames, with some hanging between the actors and the audience, so the audience can use its imagination to create the paintings.

Cast

Adele: a painter. She is dressed for the opening reception for her art show.

Boyd: a seeker. He is dressed for a job interview.

Andrew Wetmore

An Opening

The opening of a show at an art gallery. ADELE, the artist, in a party dress, is standing, studying the paintings. She moves slowly from one to another.

ADELE
No. No, just doesn't work.

BOYD ENTERS uncertainly. Looks at Adele, then around at the paintings.

ADELE
Unformed, unfocussed. Unbelievable. Unlovable.

BOYD
Me?

ADELE
Oh!

BOYD
Are you talking to me?

ADELE
No.

BOYD
Or about me?

ADELE
Why would I?

BOYD
That's what I'm thinking. But then I'm thinking, why would you say those hard things about anyone?

ADELE
I didn't realize I was speaking aloud.

> *A painting catches Boyd's eye. He glances at it, then looks more carefully. Purses his lips, then turns back to Adele.*

BOYD
Are you one of those tough-love personal trainers? You know, "I'm ripping the skin off your cheeks so you can grow better skin."

ADELE
Never.

BOYD
Because, in my experience, you don't change people that way. You just scar them.

ADELE
Do I know you?

BOYD
If we knew each other, would I have to guess what you do for a living? What do you do for a living?

ADELE
I paint.

BOYD
Not houses.

ADELE
Sometimes, as part of the composition—oh, I see. No.

BOYD
Good to hear you can make a living at that.

ADELE
I didn't say I made a living. I do it for a living. If I didn't do it, I wouldn't be alive, no matter what money I had.

BOYD
So...are you a kept woman?

ADELE
Sometimes. Sometimes I get loose for a bit.

BOYD
And when you get loose, that's when you really paint, right?

ADELE
It helps. It helps. What are you, a critic?

BOYD
Can you make a living at it?

ADELE
You can make a killing at it.

BOYD
Really.

ADELE
Of other people. Of their reputations. Of their hopes.

BOYD
Have you been killed?

ADELE
Often. Usually right before I go back to being kept. So what do you think?

BOYD
Of...?

ADELE
Forget it. If I have to ask, I won't like the answer.

BOYD
What do I think of...you? Not qualified to say very much yet.

ADELE
Great.

BOYD
Smart, funny, brave. I dunno.

ADELE
How about "none of the above"?

BOYD
You're harsh on compliments you get given. But there's an art to taking them, too.

ADELE
You were right before. You're not qualified to say.

BOYD
Yet.

> *Adele turns away and fusses with the snack table. Boyd studies a painting. Adele turns back to him.*

ADELE
Are you—is there something you want?

BOYD
Somebody said there was an opening here.

ADELE
Well, yes. Or there was. I guess there still is.

BOYD
Well, good.

ADELE
I guess. I expected more of a response.

BOYD
From me? I just heard about it.

ADELE
From the universe. Not the turnout I had hoped for. There's even leftover cheese and crackers.

BOYD
Well...is that cheese really left over?

ADELE
Help yourself.

> *BOYD moves to the snack table.*

BOYD
On the bright side, you won't have to cook this evening.

ADELE
I was thinking more of a liquid supper.

BOYD
When life gives you lemons, make limoncello?

ADELE
If only.

BOYD
I know a good recipe. Had lots of chances to refine it, as life keeps delivering the lemons.

ADELE
And this works for you?

BOYD
It's all facade. If I stop moving forward, I'll just fall down, right?

ADELE
Moving forward toward what?

BOYD
Right now, toward this opening, I guess. I mean, I'm certain! Just one more bit of cheese...haven't eaten all day.

ADELE
So, the opening.

BOYD
Yes? I mean, yes!

ADELE
What do you think?

BOYD
I'm enthusiastic and capable and, uh...What do I think about what?

ADELE
Don't get to many openings do you?

BOYD
I go after every one I find. But they're pretty scarce.

ADELE
Wait, what?

BOYD
Look, I come from here, grew up here. But I've been away for a while pursuing great success. Ontario, Alberta: you know the story.

ADELE
And?

BOYD
And great success got clean away from me. Couldn't catch it no matter how hard I ran. And I decided it was time to come home before I had run so far after success that I couldn't. Come home, I mean. But here, back home...you have to run hard just to find a, a tray of cheese, much less great success.

ADELE
But what does that have to do with going to openings?

BOYD
I hear about an opening, I go check it out. If I know what it's for, I try to tart up my resume to match it—you know, pump up this skill, hide that one. And if it's just a chance thing, like the guy at the restaurant saying there's an opening here, I take my heart in both hands and walk right in.

ADELE
To apply for the opening.

BOYD
And one day—maybe this day—it'll work. I'll get the job. These grapes help a lot with the dryness of the cheese.

ADELE
This is an art opening.

BOYD
And?

ADELE
"And?"?

BOYD
What's it involve? I betcha I can do it. Selling art, cleaning art, guarding art, transporting art—

ADELE
Showing art.

BOYD
Showing art.

ADELE
And other people buying it. Even if they didn't do much buying this time.

BOYD
Showing art.

> *He looks around at the art. Accusingly:*

BOYD
It's an art show.

ADELE
Yes. Sorry.

BOYD
Well, why the heck would they say there's an opening?

ADELE
There is one. The opening of the show. A sort of party.

> *Pause.*

BOYD
That's no fair. That's deceptive.

ADELE
That's what it's called.

BOYD
It's sneaky. And now I've eaten all this cheese for nothing. No, well, the cheese was fine, but what the hell am I doing here? There's no job.

ADELE
I'm sorry.

> *Boyd paces.*

BOYD
It's not your fault, anyhow. My stupid fault, I guess. What about you?

ADELE
Me?

BOYD
Yeah. How'd they rope you into this? You the caterer? Because

when I said the cheese was dry—

ADELE
No, no.

BOYD
Receptionist? Not much to recept right now. Except me.

ADELE
No.

BOYD
Security? Because this stuff must be worth a bomb.

ADELE
I'm the art.

BOYD
You're the art?

ADELE
Well, not the *art* art. But I'm the artist.

BOYD
This is your stuff? Oh, my God: you said you painted to live.

ADELE
Yup.

    Boyd stares around wildly at the paintings.

BOYD
All yours? All of it?

ADELE
It's my show. Of my art.

BOYD
Holy cats.

ADELE
Is it that bad?
BOYD
What? No—oh, no. Why would you think this is bad?

ADELE
The people today: they drifted in, they talked to each other, they nibbled at the food, they glanced at the art, they drifted out again.

BOYD
What about your friends?

ADELE
Those *were* my friends.

BOYD
They must be nuts. This stuff is—oh, I know what's up.

ADELE
What?

BOYD
Your buddies there, they're in the same fix I'm in. They look, and they see this amazing stuff, and they don't know how to talk about it. They didn't go to art school, I bet they don't know what words to use that won't make you laugh or insult you. Which is where I am right now.

ADELE
Insulting me?

Andrew Wetmore

BOYD
Trying not to. I don't want to use words that, well, aren't up to what I see.

ADELE
It can't be worse than saying nothing at all.

BOYD
No? All right, then. But you're going to roll your eyes.

ADELE
I promise I won't.

BOYD
Remember, the closest I usually come to art is that Bob Ross guy on TV—there you go, rolling your eyes!

ADELE
Sorry sorry sorry!

> *She covers her eyes.*

ADELE
I'm ready for you now, uh...

BOYD
Boyd.

ADELE
I'm Adele. Please try to tell me about my art, Boyd. My eyes are ready for you now.

BOYD
Your paintings are...pretty.

> *Adele snorts, then recovers.*

BOYD
Kidding, kidding. Seriously now...
(looking around)
They, they make me feel...this has not been a good time for me. Coming home but not to the home I left. I don't know. Money running short. The bills...You have to be in a tough place to want to just apply for any opening, sight unseen. So I come in here, I come in here under a misunderstanding, or that guy at the restaurant was playing a joke on me. And I come in here and look around...and I feel better. The world feels better. I want to look at these painting and, I don't know, spend some time with them. They make me feel better than I was, that things are different than they were, richer than they were.

Pause. Adele takes her hand off her eyes.

ADELE
Thank you. Things are better for me, now, too.

BOYD
Well. Good. I'll come back another day. Just to look some more.

ADELE
Wait. There might be an opening.

BOYD
I know. You said.

ADELE
No, a job. But I don't know if you would want to—

BOYD
I would. What is it?

Andrew Wetmore

ADELE
There are life drawing classes here—

BOYD
Life drawing. Like flowers?

ADELE
Like people. Naked people. And they need models. One of their regular models just moved to Alberta.

BOYD
Me? Naked, in a room full of people?

ADELE
Yeah, well, I thought you wouldn't—

BOYD
No, I can do that. That's the very first thing I did the day I was born. Does it pay?

ADELE
Yeah. Not a king's ransom, but—

BOYD
(undoing his belt)
Is there, like, an audition?

ADELE
Stop, stop! Please. I'm sure you are completely suitable. Let's go find the coordinator and talk to her about it. And...thank you.

BOYD
How about that. An opening. Hey, thank you, Adele!

ADELE
Bring the cheese plate, if you want.

BOYD
No, nope. Not if everybody's going to be watching my waistline.

   They EXIT.

END

Andrew Wetmore

Compliments of the House

Time
Now

Setting
The breakfast room of a chain motel. There is a serve-yourself counter and a couple of breakfast tables with chairs.

Cast

Lucy: a teen who yearns

Al: a travelling salesman

Adele: a server in the breakfast room

Joe: a rambler, around 18

Andrew Wetmore

Compliments of the House

The breakfast room of a chain motel. There is a serve-yourself counter and a couple of breakfast tables with chairs. LUCY, a teen, sits at a table, with her phone and an untouched plate of food. AL, a travelling salesman, has breakfast at another table.
   ADELE, a staffer, ENTERS with a tray and approaches Lucy.

ADELE
You done with that?

LUCY
I didn't start it yet.

ADELE
It'll be cold by now. I'll bus that and you can get a fresh plate.

LUCY
Maybe I like congealed eggs.

ADELE
Then you come to the wrong place.

   She takes the plate before Lucy can stop her.

LUCY
You're not my mom!

ADELE
Lucky for you.

> *As Adele EXITS, JOE, a young man, ENTERS, avoiding her eyes. He scans the room. Approaches the food warily, but hungrily. Lucy sneaks a glance. Joe grabs a mini muffin and stuffs it in his mouth. Grabs another and an apple and puts them in his jacket pockets. Looks around. Takes a plate and starts to fill it with food.*
>   *Adele ENTERS with a fresh carafe of coffee.*

ADELE
Excuse me....Excuse me.

JOE
(mouth full)
Yeff?

ADELE
Are you a guest here?

JOE
Mrpmh, flffp mmm hoff.

ADELE
Because this breakfast is compliments of the house for our guests. Only our guests.

LUCY
Tommy, Stop harassing the staff.

JOE
Uh wuffn't--

LUCY
You always.
(to Adele)

My brother thinks because he's a star athlete and gets these high grades he can dress like a rag bin and nobody will say boo.

ADELE
This is your brother?

LUCY
(crossing to them)
All the brothers I have.

    Punches Joe playfully on the arm.

LUCY
Whatcha gonna eat?

JOE
(after swallowing)
...Everything?

    Lucy hands him a plate, takes one herself.

LUCY
Once mom and dad get down here it'll be all hurry hurry up, so let's eat before they tell us to.

JOE
Okay...

LUCY
Mom will say, "Lucy, you need more protein and less sugar." As if.

JOE
She's probably right...Lucy.

LUCY
I don't recommend the eggs.

ADELE
They were fine until you ignored them.
> *She leaves the carafe and EXITS.*

JOE
What are you doing?

LUCY
What are *you* doing? No, wait. Get your food and join me. Tell me there. That will look more normal.

> *She returns to the table and sits with her back to him. Joe looks toward the exit door.*

LUCY
Don't even think of it.

> *Joe starts to fill his plate.*

LUCY
I'm not normally up this early—as you would know if you were really my brother. But things got tense last night and I just could not sleep.

JOE
"Things"?

LUCY
Mom and dad fighting about me. Again.

> *Joe joins her at the table, eats quickly.*

JOE
Are they, you know, real? Or more of whatever performance you're performing?

LUCY
Solid, respectable, proper, very real. Righteous.

JOE
I should get going, then.

LUCY
Eat. I went out on a limb for those carbs.

JOE
So, about that—

LUCY
Don't talk with your mouth full, Tommy.

JOE
What game is this? And I'm Joe.

LUCY
You'll always be Tommy to me. You owe me. Tommy.

JOE
All I want is a little food, then I'll be on my way.

LUCY
To what?

JOE
To the next thing. Whatever.

LUCY
What do you do?

JOE
I can fix cars. Washing machines. Chimneys. I can dig a ditch. I can

pound in fence posts. I can cook better eggs than these.

LUCY
I warned you. So why—?

JOE
Out of work, out of money, so out of food. It happens.

LUCY
My dad says poor people just don't want to work.

JOE
What does he do?

LUCY
He mainly takes clients to lunch, I think.

>   *She puts up a warning hand as Adele ENTERS.*

LUCY
So, you think you'll make the varsity this year?

JOE
What? Oh. Maybe. If I can just...

>   *Mimes throwing a football.*

LUCY
Basketball team.

JOE
...get my one-handed, fade-away jump shot working.

LUCY
The recruiters will be fan-girling all over you.

Adele, having checked the food table, EXITS.

LUCY
You're not local, Tommy. Or she'd recognize you.

JOE
Joe. I'm just passing through.

LUCY
Joe. Passing through to where?

JOE
Some place with work and no trouble.

LUCY
Take me with you.

JOE
What? Why?

LUCY
"Why?"? Look at me, Joe. I'm the best offer you'll get all day.

JOE
You're already going somewhere. With your family.

LUCY
They hate me.

JOE
Look at you, Lucy. They don't hate you.

LUCY
They're going to dump me back at boarding school so they can fight with each other in peace.

Andrew Wetmore

JOE
"Boarding school."

LUCY
Oop.

JOE
You're like twelve years old.

LUCY
I'm totally legal. Or I will be before they catch up with us.

JOE
Lucy—

LUCY
In Nigeria the age of consent is 11, so maybe we can go there.

JOE
You've researched this?

LUCY
Everybody checks that out. Italy is 14, if you like pizza.

JOE
You want to go to Nigeria with someone you don't know in order to not go to boarding school where you have a great education, hot meals, and no scorpions?

LUCY
Scorpions!

JOE
(standing)
Patch it up with your folks, whatever it is.

LUCY
Take a step toward the door and I will cry rape.

Joe sits. Lucy drops a wallet on the table.

LUCY
I have money. I can pay my way.

JOE
You boosted your dad's wallet?

LUCY
He'll think it was the cleaning crew.

JOE
I'm not for sale.

LUCY
I already bought you.

JOE
I am worth more than a muffin!

LUCY
What if I said they beat me? Locked me in my room?

JOE
Do they?

LUCY
You would rescue me, right?

JOE
(standing)
No.

LUCY
What's wrong with me?

JOE
Nothing. You're perfect.

LUCY
But—

JOE
I'm not that guy. The strange guy you throw yourself at is never that guy. This is not a movie.

LUCY
But I saved you.

JOE
I am not your ride.

LUCY
Why not?

JOE
Got no car, for one thing..

LUCY
Tommy!

JOE
Joe.

    Adele ENTERS with her tray.

ADELE
Everything all right?

LUCY
No.

JOE
Yes.

ADELE
Siblings.

LUCY
Tommy is a jerk.

JOE
Lucy is...
(catches himself)
The best sister I could ever have.

LUCY
Yeah, right. Don't give me that—what?

ADELE
Ain't they sweet? Too bad she don't know from eggs.

    She EXITS.

LUCY
Last chance, Joe. Take me with you.

JOE
Every time I eat a muffin, I will think of you.

LUCY
That is a gross thing to say.

JOE
I gotta go find a fence post to pound. Make me proud of you.

    He EXITS.

LUCY
(calling after him)
How will you know? If I do do good, how will you know?

AL
I got wheels.

LUCY
What?

AL
You need a ride. I can take you.

LUCY
I wasn't talking to you.

AL
That guy, Joe, he didn't listen to you. I listened.

He stands, crosses to her.

AL
I'll give you a ride you'll never forget.

LUCY
No you won't.

AL
I got what you want, little girl. Take you right out of your boring life.

LUCY
Creep.

AL
Playin' hard to get? I can dig that.

He grabs her wrist. She tries to pull away.

AL
Joe ain't going to bail you out. It's just you and me.

Adele ENTERS with her serving tray.

ADELE
Your meal's over there, sir.

AL
Yeah, but my dessert is right here.

Adele swings her tray, hits Al across the back of the head. He staggers, falls.

LUCY
What? *What?*

ADELE
Oh, dear. I think he fainted. I'll throw some water on him once you're gone.

LUCY
How did you know?

ADELE
Thin walls in this crap place. I heard every word.

LUCY
Even—?

ADELE
Yeah, you and your "brother" and all.

LUCY
Oh, God.

ADELE
If you just et your eggs none of this would have happened.

LUCY
They're all jerks.

ADELE
Don't blame that Joe. He was right not to take you along. This guy? Yes, capital J erk.

LUCY
I'm just...I'm just gonna go back up. To our room.

She grabs up the wallet; heads for the door. Turns back.

LUCY
He could've...I could've...Thank you.

ADELE
That school you're going to. Do they make you write essays? Like "How I spent my summer vacation"?

LUCY
They do, yeah.

ADELE
Now you got the material you need for a real page-turner. Compliments of the house.

BLACKOUT

One-Minute Warning

Time
Now

Setting
The HR office in a major corporation. A desk, a couple of chairs.

Cast

Jen: an HR staffer

Leon: a software developer

James: an intern

Andrew Wetmore

One-Minute Warning

> *An office: a desk, a couple of chairs. JEN is on the phone. LEON is standing at a distance, looking out over the audience.*

JEN
(to the phone)
I see all the KRAs are complete except for your team's....Well, 90% is not complete, I'm sorry.
(to Leon)
I won't be long.
(to the phone)
I know the deadline isn't dead yet. But all the other teams have their KRAs submitted...Why would I threaten you? I was just pointing out...Okay, well get them in as soon as—okay, bye.
(to Leon, as she hangs up)
People are so touchy, you know? I'm just doing my job, helping them do their job. You know? Leon?

LEON
Oh, sorry. I was thinking.

JEN
Well, we can't have that around here!

> *Leon is puzzled.*

JEN
Joke. That's a joke. Just a sec.

She picks up phone, pushes a number;

JEN
James, could you step in, please? Yes, now.
(to Leon, as she hangs up)
Maybe we should have people raise their hands or something when they tell a joke so the other people can be sure.

LEON
Is that also a joke?

JEN
Some people just don't get each other. And then they come crying to HR. I am not their nanny!

LEON
No. You are their human resource.

JEN
I am HR for the company. Hiring and firing. Policy. Oh, and policy enforcement. Why do people get the idea that I'm here to serve people?

LEON
A foolish error.

JEN
That was probably unprofessional of me. Was it?

LEON
Extremely.

JEN
Oh, no! Oh, I'm sorry!

Leon raises his hand.

JEN
What? Ah, that was a joke.

LEON
Evidently not.

JEN
Well, I won't complain about your jokes if you just, um, forget about my little rant.

JAMES steps into the room. He has one hand behind his back.

JEN
Hello, James. Leon, you know James.

LEON
No.

JAMES
Hello.

LEON
Now I do.

JEN
I asked James to step in to help with our little chat. Please, sit down.

LEON
I can stand.

JEN
Funny thing, that's exactly the issue. You. Standing.

LEON
Me.

JEN
You. Standing.

LEON
I admit it. I do stand.

JEN
From what I read here...this was on the fifth floor, not your floor. You were walking, just normal I suppose, And then suddenly you weren't.

LEON
Normal?

JEN
Walking. You were just standing there, for a very long time. And then you started walking again.

LEON
And then...?

JEN
And then you walked away, I guess.

LEON
I'm not sure I—

JEN
People were worried.

LEON
"People"?

JEN
Two people. They thought you had a stroke or something.

LEON
But they didn't come over to see.

JEN
They were freaked out. And by the time they decided--

LEON
I had walked away.

JEN
Which freaked them out more.

LEON
Really.

JEN
What it says, right here. "Freaked out".

LEON
These would be younger people.

JEN
You shouldn't make age-ist remarks.

LEON
That was a language remark—

JEN
Younger people have rights. And older people sometimes trample on them.

LEON
Are you speaking as a younger person?

JEN
I'm speaking as a certified Human Resourcer. And "freaked out" probably totally describes how they felt.

LEON
Totally.

JEN
Leon, I think the art of business involves not annoying other people. Not mocking the way they speak.

LEON
Sorry.

JEN
Not acting in odd ways near other people's cubicles. Or in your own cubicle, for that matter: your co-cubists have rights, too! So I've asked James to give you a hand in the short term while we work on this issue. James is going to shadow you in the office, and when he notices you, well, just standing there, he's going to give you a bit of a jog.

LEON
A bit of a jog?

JEN
So you don't start to freak people out. James?

> *James produces and uses a loud noise-maker, anything from an air-horn to cymbals.*

JEN
Thank you.

LEON
And when will he do this?

JEN
James?

JAMES
Any time after one minute of inaction, sir.

JEN
I think after a week or two you will start reminding yourself, and James will not be necessary.

LEON
And James doing that will not freak out my co-cubists?

JEN
I'll have a quiet word with them.

LEON
What if I'm thinking about a work-related issue?

JEN
This is the twenty-first century. What could possibly take more than a minute to think out?

> *Leon hesitates, starts to speak a couple of times. James brings out his noise maker.*

LEON
Down, James. I'm not pausing. I'm just at a loss for words.

JEN
We would not take this step if it was not a serious issue.

LEON
Thinking is different from speed dating.

JEN
Speed dating gets results. What does your "thinking" get?

LEON
Insight? Wisdom? Balance?

JEN
But what we need is results.

LEON
"Ready, fire, aim"?

JAMES
That's sort of funny.

The others look at him.

JAMES
Sorry.

JEN
It doesn't help productivity to distract others and affect their work negatorily.

LEON
You're doing that on purpose, aren't you?

JEN
Now, let's talk about these pausing incidents. This one was last month.

LEON
That narrows it down.

JEN
This was on...the eleventh.

LEON
November 11. Eleven minutes past eleven in the morning.

JEN
Interesting that you should remember so exactly.

LEON
Of course I remember exactly. It is...memorable.

JEN
Is that what you want? To be memorable?

LEON
Me? No. November 11, at 11 minutes past 11—that's memorable.

JEN
Should I know why?

LEON
Yes.

JEN
Oh, wait. That's, um...no, that September 11. Silly me. So what's this November one about?

LEON
It's about 40 million people dead or wounded—blown to bits, drowned in flooded trenches, frozen in the winter war. And how many more lives distorted, stunted, by the loss of a father, or their town erased from the map—

Andrew Wetmore

JEN
What? When?

LEON
And on the 11th of November, 1918, just past eleven o'clock, the great powers signed an agreement that ended the Great War. You've heard about the Great War.

JEN
Not as such.

LEON
No. You may know it as World War I.

JEN
Oh! Oh, yes. That.

LEON
So, on that day and at that hour, I stop what I'm doing for a minute and remember those who fought and died, who suffered, who—

JEN
Why?

LEON
Because they're—memorable.

JEN
Do you think this helps them?

LEON
It helps me, at any rate, to remember them.

JEN
Does it help you be a better software engineer?

LEON
It helps me not get into cataclysmic conflicts.

JEN
Do you find yourself wanting to get into fights?

> *Leon raises his hand.*

JEN
Oh. Ha ha. Couldn't you honour them with a minute sometime after work? Because this is a forward-looking company, right? We can't get as forwarder as we want to, if key people are spending time looking backward.

LEON
How do you know the path forward unless you look at where you've been? You could be walking into the same mistakes that—

JEN
We don't make mistakes—

LEON
There will always be—

JEN
That is backward-looking thinking! We have policies and procedures that cover every option and interaction of our normal daily work. We are 9001 compliant! Therefore, no more mistakes.

LEON
Were your parents very critical?

JEN
What?

LEON
Did they have unrealistic expectations for you?

JEN
This is not about me! It is about you totally freaking people out. This doesn't just happen on November Whatsit.

LEON
Eleven.

JEN
Eleven. I have gathered some other sightings.

LEON
Sightings?

JEN
People seeing you—pause.

LEON
People seeing me pause and complaining?

JEN
This is a pro-activated HR department. We don't have to wait for complaints. What about last week? December 8.

JAMES
I know that one: John Lennon got shot.

JEN
Oh.

JAMES
(sings)
"Imagine there's no heaven--"

JEN
Thank you, James. OK: the day before. December 7.

LEON
Pearl Harbor Day.

Jen is blank.

LEON
1941: The Japanese launched a sneak attack, destroying the US Pacific fleet and killing thousands of people.

JEN
Okay, okay. Worth remembering. But for crying out loud, there's one every day! December 6.

LEON
In 1989 a man walked into a lecture hall in a technical college in Montreal, forced the male students to leave, and shot the women.

JEN
What?

LEON
Shot 23 women and four men. Killed 14 of the women.

JEN
But why?

Leon takes out a file card, hands it to Jen.

LEON
He didn't like uppity women. Each December 6 I speak the list of the dead women's names. It probably takes more than a minute, James. I remember them because, when someone tells me to leave

so he can shoot people, I want to remember not to leave. I want to remember to try and stop him.

JEN
But...but...

LEON
You say we're a forward-looking company. But there is backwardness all around. I try to remember that each day.

JEN
Those women...

LEON
Anyhow, I have to get back to being productive...

JEN
Oh. Oh, yes. Of course. Of course.

LEON
Okay, then. Walk this way, James.

> *Leon EXITS.*

JAMES
Wait!

> *He EXITS quickly.*
> *Jen takes the file card. She looks around, then stands up. Looks around. Reads.*

JEN
Geneviève Bergeron. Hélène Colgan...Nathalie Croteau... Barbara Daigneault.

> *Pause. She wipes at her eyes.*

JEN
Anne-Marie Edward...Maud Haviernick. Maryse...Maryse Laganière...

> *Puts down the card. Picks up the phone.*

JEN
Please...please find James for me, the intern. I want him to stop doing what I told him to do. I'll find him something else to do...Something productive, yes.

> *She hangs up; picks up the card again.*

JEN
Anne-Marie Lemay...Sonia Pelletier...Michèle Richard...

> *Blackout*

END

Andrew Wetmore

Quiet Car

Time
Now

Setting
North Station in Boston. If you choose a station closer to where you are, there is a line you need to adjust.

Cast

Bill: a man in his forties

Sally: a woman in her twenties.

Passengers just off a commuter train.

Andrew Wetmore

Quiet Car

North Station in Boston. BILL walks from the platform into the waiting room; looks up at the board announcing trains. Starts to walk off.
  SALLY appears behind him.

SALLY
Wait!

Bill hesitates, then continues.

SALLY
Please wait!

Bill turns.

SALLY
I just want to talk to you.

BILL
Talk?

SALLY
Talk. With you.

BILL
Why?

SALLY
Does that seem so strange? We see each other every day...

BILL
I have to—

SALLY
Why don't you want to talk to me? You look at me.

BILL
Me?

SALLY
Of course you do. Every day, in the Quiet Car.

BILL
In the—

SALLY
On the train. You know we sit in the Quiet Car, don't you? So I can't talk to you there.

BILL
I didn't know.

SALLY
You didn't know you always look at me?

BILL
I didn't know it was the Quiet Car.

SALLY
Why are you making this so hard? I just want to talk to you.

BILL
Let's go over here.

SALLY
Why?

BILL
To talk. Out of the way of people.

They move DL together.

SALLY
Why do you want to be out of the way?

BILL
Why do you want to talk?

SALLY
Because—you look at me. I want to know why.

BILL
Does there have to be a "why"?

SALLY
Nobody looks at me. Just you.

BILL
That cannot be true.

SALLY
If I'm not holding the snacks, nobody looks at me. I thought I was used to it. But then I found you looking at me.

BILL
I'm sorry.

SALLY
You don't get it, do you? Why should you be sorry?

Andrew Wetmore

BILL
I was intruding.

SALLY
It's okay—

BILL
As you are intruding.

SALLY
Oh. Sorry.

>   *Beat.*

SALLY
This is where you say, 'It's okay.'

BILL
I have to go.

SALLY
Go where? I don't think you have anywhere to go to.

BILL
Excuse me.

SALLY
I followed you last Friday.

BILL
No.

SALLY
I got on the train, in the Quiet Car, like always. You got on and sat down. You watched me. You didn't say anything—

BILL
It is the Quiet Car.

SALLY
D'oh. Then we all got off here at North Station. And then—

BILL
Stop.

SALLY
You got on another train. Going to some nowhere on another line. So I got on behind you.

BILL
I did not see you.

SALLY
You sat down in a talky-talky car, but you didn't talk to anybody. I sat down just behind you. You didn't look at anybody.

BILL
I cannot.

SALLY
But I started to think, what if he gets off at some nowhere and I get off to see what he does, and he doesn't do anything but stand there? And there we are on this nowhere platform, just us two until the next train comes by. It's what you do, right?

BILL
Not...always.

SALLY
That would be awkward. So I got off again before the train left.

BILL
Why should you follow me? Why is it your business?

SALLY
You watch me. Gives me a right to watch you. Doesn't it?

BILL
You should not follow me.

SALLY
Then who should I follow?

BILL
Someone who—someone who...

SALLY
Someone who has somewhere to go to?

BILL
I have places to go to. Going is always good.

SALLY
"To travel hopefully is a better thing than to arrive." Do you know who said that?

BILL
I don't travel hopefully.

SALLY
Robert Louis Stevenson, the writer. I know lots of interesting things. I can tell them to you all morning.

BILL
You have to go to work.

SALLY
They don't care. I don't care. So, which of Robert Louis Stevenson's books do you want to know about? I've only read "Kidnapped", myself; but there's "Dr Jeckyl and--"

BILL
Please.

SALLY
You're right. You know, if I didn't sit in the Quiet Car, I'd be talking away the whole ride. Probably nobody would sit with me, so I'd be talking to myself—

BILL
People sit with you.

SALLY
They sit beside me, not with me. They'd sit on me, if I didn't say 'hey!' You look at me because I remind you of somebody, right?

BILL
No.

SALLY
Your wife who ran away with the gutter cleaning guy. Or a dear cousin, from whom you now are estranged. Or—

BILL
You don't remind me of anybody.

SALLY
But—

BILL
Not anybody. Your face is just random features to me.

Andrew Wetmore

SALLY
That's why you look at me all the time? No way.

BILL
It is the way. If I close my eyes I see them.

SALLY
"Them"?

BILL
If I look in other faces in the train, I see them.

SALLY
Who are they?

BILL
They do not leave me alone.

SALLY
Okay...

BILL
You must have those moments, when a memory leaps from the back of your mind and makes you flinch?

SALLY
What I do in the shower is my own business.

BILL
Think how would it be if that happened every minute. A red wire of memory. From each face you look on. So it is for me. Except when I look on you.

SALLY
So I'm like, white noise for your eyes?

BILL
I'm sorry.

SALLY
A blur. A test pattern.

BILL
Not a blur. A blur would not help.

SALLY
I'm not a blur. Nicest thing I've heard all week.

BILL
You are young. Your pains are the pains of the young. You will see.

SALLY
How old are you?

BILL
A thousand years old.

SALLY
Oh. So, how was drama class?

BILL
What?

SALLY
You aren't that old. Not old enough to snob it over me. "Nobody knows da trubbel I seen—"

BILL
I meant no—

SALLY
I wasn't comparing our sorrows, anyway. I haven't said word one

about my sorrows.

BILL
You said they don't care if you come to work.

SALLY
Oh, yeah: I did. And they don't. And it pisses me off. But it has nothing to do with my wanting to talk to you.

BILL
Of course it does.

SALLY
I don't need to talk to anybody about the people at work. They aren't exactly the stuff of dreams.

BILL
The stuff of dreams is...unspeakable.

SALLY
You got to get better dreams.

BILL
You do not know the dreams I have.

SALLY
I can get you better dreams. "We are such stuff as dreams are made on", ya know. Not the other way around. And that's another quote.

BILL
The elements of the dream, they mix and remix. But the faces boil up at me again and again. When I look on any other face than yours.

SALLY
What's in the dream?

BILL
A class reunion. A hayride on a twisty road, thirty happy people and the farmer, driving north toward a beach. A log truck heading south on the same road, very fast. A young driver. The hairpin turn. Everything moving so slow and so fast, all at the same time. The faces. The faces.

SALLY
Oh, God. You were the driver.

BILL
I was the one who stayed home. Who thought a hay ride would be boring. I am the one to whom nothing happened.

SALLY
You need new dreams.

BILL
You think we choose our dreams?

SALLY
Come walk with me.

BILL
I have to—

SALLY
We can walk all over Boston. I know some great walks. I can fill your eyes with new things, dreamy new things.

BILL
The old dreams do not let go.

SALLY
I can walk backwards in front of you, so you can look at me.

BILL
Why would you do that?

SALLY
I like you to look at me. And maybe, if you look long enough...

BILL
Yes?

SALLY
My face will start to remind you of someone after all.

BILL
But that is--

SALLY
It'll remind you of me, silly.

BILL
Why...?

SALLY
Why what?

BILL
Why do you sit in the quiet car? You are full of talk.

SALLY
It was a mistake the first time. I was chattin' away, not that anybody listens—nobody ever listens. And the conductor stifled me. I was ready to move out, but then I saw you looking at me. And the next day you looked at me again. So the quiet car it is. I figure: he looks at me, maybe in time he'll listen to me.

BILL
You don't know me.

SALLY
Gee, I wonder how we fix that?

BILL
When you know me—if you knew me, you would not want me to look on you.

SALLY
We're going to give it a try, okay? I'm Sally.

BILL
...Bill.

SALLY
See? Miles of progress already. Stroll or coffee shop?

BILL
Well...

SALLY
Or something wilder?

BILL
There is...

SALLY
Yes?

BILL
There is a train to Rockport. We can just make it.

SALLY
Rockport? What's in Rockport? And don't say 'rocks'.

BILL
The journey has a good rhythm; there are some pleasing views. The return trip starts always on time.

SALLY
And can we sit in the talky-talky car? And actually talk?

BILL
Yes. Okay. If I can look on you.

SALLY
Deal! All aboard, Bill.

> *He awkwardly gestures toward a platform. She takes his hand and walks backwards ahead of him as they EXIT.*

BLACKOUT
END

Fig

Based on Genesis chapter 2.

Time
The beginning of the world.

Setting
Just outside the Garden of Eden

Cast

Adam: the first man

Eve: the first woman

Andrew Wetmore

Fig

ADAM and EVE are picking ineptly at fig leaves, making clothing.

ADAM
Don't you *ever* listen to a snake again.

EVE
You named it. Why didn't you put a sign on it?

ADAM
"Ssssnaaaakkke" isn't enough of a warning?

EVE
Obviously not.

ADAM
All you had to do is not listen to it.

EVE
How was I supposed to know that? I could listen to anything else I wanted to in the Garden. Besides, it said a lot of true things. It's not my fault that a smart snake could...could...word, please.

ADAM
"Suborn"?

EVE
"Suborn"??

ADAM
"To induce or instigate another to do something illegal."

EVE
All right. It's not my fault the snake could suborn me. I didn't have any experience in, in...

ADAM
Duplicity: "hypocritical cunning or deception."

EVE
Thank you. What did I know about duplicity?

ADAM
You knew where that apple came from when you offered it to me.

EVE
So did you.

ADAM
How could I know that?

EVE
You looked at it. You smelled it. You *knew*.

ADAM
I trusted you.

EVE
It's not my fault you trusted me. Why should I be more reliable than a snake?

ADAM
I think we're supposed to be.

EVE
I didn't just force you to eat it, you know. I tasted it first, to protect you. The snake said I wouldn't die if I ate it, and I didn't.

ADAM
Not yet.

EVE
You're going to hold this over me forever, aren't you?

ADAM
Only as long as you live.

EVE
Anyhow, Mr. fig-leaf-sewing-man, unless you get a move on, I am going to die of, of...

ADAM
Chagrin? "Feeling of disappointment, humiliation, embarrassment caused by failure or discomfiture."

EVE
No.

ADAM
Logorrhea. "Excessive talkativeness."

EVE
No!

ADAM
Exposure: "Being unprotected or uncovered."

Andrew Wetmore

EVE
That's the one. It was never chilly like this in the Garden.

ADAM
It's tough to sew fig leaves together when needles have not been invented yet.

EVE
You're just one great big ball of excuses.

ADAM
I gave you a skirt. It's not my fault you have more parts to feel chagrin about than I do.

EVE
Oh, and that's my fault, too?

ADAM
That was the take-away message I got.

EVE
Oh, right. He made us. And he said we were "very good." I heard him.

ADAM
And were you listening to him when he kicked us out?

EVE
It wasn't my fault. It was the snake's fault.

ADAM
And where is that snake? My shorts could use a nice belt.

EVE
You're the one who names things. Name a place for the snake and that's where it'll be.

ADAM
It doesn't work that way.

EVE
Excuses, excuses.

ADAM
What was wrong with Macintoshes? Or Golden Deliciouses?

EVE
Would any other fruit make us like gods, knowing good and evil?

ADAM
I didn't want to know evil.

EVE
You always want to know everything. It's not my fault you don't like what you found this time.

ADAM
If it wasn't for you, I'd still be in the Garden.

EVE
You don't know that. You'd have found a way to mess up.

ADAM
There was one rule. Don't eat from this tree.

EVE
If you only have one rule, how can you learn about rules? We should have had some small rules we could practice on. He never gave me a chance to become, become...

ADAM
Manipulative? "Managing artfully or by a shrewd use of influence, especially in an unfair way."

EVE
Watch it.

ADAM
Proficient? "Highly competent; skilled."

EVE
Close enough. I didn't get a chance to be proficient at rules. It's not fair.

ADAM
What was unfair? He said, don't eat or there will be trouble. It was you who ate—

EVE
You ate, too.

ADAM
You had already bitten it. I didn't want it to go to waste.

EVE
What you should have done is hidden us better.

ADAM
Hidden better from God?

EVE
Oh, you're so smart now. But all you could think of then was hide behind a tree. You could have named yourself a bush, and me a stump, and we wouldn't have had to go through all this.

ADAM
It doesn't work that way.

EVE
How do you know? You never tried.

ADAM
Watch, then: "Eve is brilliant and thoughtful." Nope, it hasn't changed a thing.

EVE
So we were doomed from the start. Doomed to fall, doomed to fail. I'm a victim of, of...

ADAM
Foolishness? "Lack of sense, unwisdom, silliness."

EVE
No!

ADAM
Circumstances? "Conditions affecting a person."

EVE
I'm a victim of circumstances!

    Beat.

ADAM
I wonder what would have happened if we had apologized.

EVE
I don't know that word.

ADAM
"Apologize: acknowledge and express regret for a fault or wrong;

to say that one is sorry."

EVE
"Apologize..." Could we have done that? I was so ashamed of my nakedness already, and he seemed pretty annoyed.

ADAM
What could he have done more than throw us out of the Garden? He might even have let us stay.

EVE
"Apologize"? "Apologize." How do you do it?

ADAM
I think...I don't know. I've never done it.

EVE
And what happens if you do do it?

ADAM
I'm not exactly sure. But I bet we'll have plenty of chances to find out. Here's your blouse.

EVE
Oh, Adam: green is not a good colour for me.

ADAM
Sorry.

EVE
Say what?

ADAM
"Sorry."

EVE
"Sorry"? Did you just—?

ADAM
I think so. Yeah. "Sorry." "I'm sorry."

EVE
Oh. Well, uh...That's all right. Don't worry about it.

ADAM
Wow. You did that elegantly.

EVE
Pretty good for a first try.

ADAM
Want a fig?

END

Andrew Wetmore

Public Humiliation

Time
Now

Setting
A hall and the kitchen in Herb and Janice's house.

Cast

Janice

Herb: her husband

Willy: Herb's brother

Andrew Wetmore

Public Humiliation

A hall in a house. JANICE is standing there, waiting. Sound of TOILET FLUSHING. HERB appears, buttoning up.

JANICE
You took your time.

HERB
You timed me?

JANICE
I normally try to avoid thinking of you when you're in there.

HERB
But this time you timed me. Is that the first time, or have I now been two-timed.

JANICE
I wanted to tell you—

HERB
Because if I know you're timing me, everything will clench up and take longer.

JANICE
I wanted to tell you--

HERB
You normally just call through the door. "How long you gonna be in

there?" "Dinner's on the table."

JANICE
Herb: Your brother's here.

HERB
My brother?

JANICE
Here.

HERB
Why?

JANICE
I wanted to ask you.

HERB
He doesn't come here.

JANICE
Which is why I'm asking.

HERB
Did someone die?

JANICE
And he's coming to break the news?

HERB
He'd come to see is he in the will.

JANICE
Well, he's here.

HERB
You said.

JANICE
What a person does when he has a visitor, he goes to greet him.

HERB
You didn't greet him?

JANICE
Of course I did.

HERB
So that part's been done. Good.

JANICE
He came to see you, not me.

HERB
Why?

JANICE
When you find out, let me know.

HERB
You're going to leave me with him? I never know what to say to him.

JANICE
Herb: once you find out what he wants, you'll know what to say. That's how it works.

HERB
Where is he?

JANICE
In the kitchen. Don't worry: I hid the knives.

> *Herb moves to the kitchen, which has a table and two chairs. WILLY is standing beside a chair.*

WILLY
Oh, you are here.

HERB
Willy.

WILLY
Then I can settle in.
(Sitting)
Didn't want to be alone in the house with your wife. She's quite a cougar, Herb.

HERB
Janice?

WILLY
She might be all over me. Frustrated housewife, looking for something more. That could be me. Because she's married to something less. That could be you.

HERB
Nonsense.

WILLY
It's the talk of the town.

HERB
You are so full of—

> *He stops as Janice enters the kitchen.*

JANICE
He's so full of what? Coffee, Willy?

WILLY
No. Thanks.

JANICE
Something stronger?

WILLY
I don't drink where I'm not welcome.

JANICE
You must be a thirsty guy. Coffee, Herb?

HERB
Uh, yes.

JANICE
You can sit down with him, you know.

HERB
I know.

WILLY
You won't sit with me, little brother?

HERB
The last time I sat down with you, it was dad's funeral.

WILLY
Yes, it was. Good times. But you didn't even come back to the house after. We had a feast ready.

HERB
(sitting)
I went to the graveyard with the ashes. Then I went home.

WILLY
Do you actually think a funeral is about the dead? You always did miss the point. A funeral—a funeral is to celebrate dodging the bullet. About being alive while another member of the herd who's gotten too slow or too sick gets cut down. A funeral, Herb: it's about the party after.

HERB
(to Janice)
How long do I have to listen?

JANICE
You're the brother. You'll know when it's enough.

HERB
The funeral was two years ago. You had to tell me this today?

WILLY
I would have told you then, but you didn't come to the after-party to be told. Like you were the dead one. But that's not why I'm here.

JANICE
(giving Herb his coffee)
Oh, there is a reason.

WILLY
Beyond your lovely rump? Yes, there is.

JANICE
Spit it out, Willy.

WILLY
(to Herb)
The nice thing about women is, when they have a thought that isn't lined up with yours, you can just ignore them.

HERB
Which is why you live alone.

WILLY
You don't know nothin'.

HERB
You don't live alone?

WILLY
I'm a breakfast-serial monogamist. I feed 'em breakfast and tell 'em goodbye.

HERB
I don't need to know.

WILLY
But you need to have an opinion.

HERB
My home, my opinions.

JANICE
You two are not at all alike. Nope.

HERB
Willy, what do you want?

WILLY
Not to be insulted by my own family. Not to be held out for ridicule. Not to be slapped in the back, uh, stabbed in the face.

JANICE
Ow.

HERB
I haven't done a thing to you.

WILLY
Liar.

HERB
(standing)
Time to leave, Willy.

WILLY
Did you, or did you didn't, unfriend me?

HERB
Did I what?

WILLY
Unfriend me. Online. For everybody to see.

JANICE
Wait. He did what?

WILLY
Unfriended. Me.

JANICE
Herb, did you unfriend him?

HERB
We're not friends, so it seemed—

WILLY
We don't have to be friends. We're family.

JANICE
Why did you unfriend him?

WILLY
Pulled down my pants in the middle of the street.

HERB
It's not the same thing.

WILLY
I know that. I was using a semaphore.

JANICE
A semaphore?

HERB
Halfway between a simile and a metaphor. His claim to fame.

JANICE
You thought that up?

WILLY
It just came to me.

JANICE
Huh.

WILLY
It's a humiliation. I got a tough enough life without my own family piling on.

HERB
Easy response, Willy: you unfriend me right back.

Andrew Wetmore

WILLY
Then how will I know what you're doing? How will you know what I'm doing?

HERB
Does either one of us care?

WILLY
It would be like having a mosquito in the room and you don't know where it is.

JANICE
You follow me, Willy. That should tell you what we're up to.

WILLY
I just follow you for the pictures.

JANICE
I know that.

HERB
What pictures?

WILLY
All of them.

HERB
You stalk my wife?

WILLY
It's clear you don't. She deserves it.

JANICE
Yeah: I'm celery, please stalk me.

WILLY
You're going to waste, and you know it.

JANICE
Look all you want, Willy. But you will never touch.
WILLY
That's what they all start out saying.

HERB
(to Janice)
Now do you see?

JANICE
See what?

HERB
Why should I have his crap in my news feed?

WILLY
Afraid of the real truth?

HERB
I don't care about what you re-post. It's what you write as your own opinions.

JANICE
He's in my news feed, too.

HERB
Cleanse thyself!

JANICE
What is wrong with you?

HERB
You like him in your feed?

Andrew Wetmore

WILLY
She likes me in her feed.

JANICE
Look, Herb. You never know when something might happen.

WILLY
Like I win the lottery.

JANICE
Or you blow your own head off. If you disappear from the news feed, I'll know we need to find out.

HERB
Why bother?

JANICE
He's family.

WILLY
I'm family.

HERB
If Hitler was family—

JANICE
He would post some pretty diverting stuff, don't you think?

HERB
I give up.

WILLY
So you're going to re-friend me?

HERB
I'm not.

WILLY
You're letting down your little wife. Like I always said. Whereas I, from time to time, might let her up.

JANICE
Willy.

WILLY
What?

JANICE
Time to go.

WILLY
Is he going to friend me again?

JANICE
Goodbye, WIlly.

WILLY
(standing)
All right then. I have just begun to fight.

    He EXITS.

JANICE
Re-friend him.

HERB
What pictures?

JANICE
You have to refriend him. Or we will never hear the end of it.

HERB
What about those pictures?

JANICE
What about them? It doesn't hurt to let him look.

HERB
Because he's family?

JANICE
You're catching on.

HERB
I want to see those pictures.

JANICE
Can't.

HERB
What? I'm more family than he is.

JANICE
Can't see them because I've blocked you.

HERB
You've what?

JANICE
Ages ago. And you never even noticed.

HERB
You blocked me? Why would you do that?

JANICE
Because you never look any more.

HERB
You can't block me. I'm your family!

JANICE
See how it feels?

                        BLACKOUT
                           END

Andrew Wetmore

At the End of My Rope

Time
Any time

Setting
The entrance to somewhere grand

Cast
One
Two
Two actors of any combination of genders

Andrew Wetmore

At the End of my Rope

> *ONE and TWO are standing outside a door, which is L. They are joined together by a rope, the ends of which are tied around their foreheads in such a way that they could be removed easily—and, of course, do not hurt the actors.*
>
> *One is standing SL, Two a little right of centre. They are as far apart from each other as the rope will allow without their having to lean away from each other. There is a chair DL which ONE can sit in if the blocking allows it; its real function is as a hitching post at the end. Alternatively, there can be some other sort of hitching post, like a coat rack.*

ONE
It's getting late.

TWO
Finally you admit it!

ONE
I don't admit anything!

> *Beat.*

ONE
Admit what?

TWO
That you're making us late.

Andrew Wetmore

ONE
It's not me who's making us late.

TWO
Almost the worst thing about you is that you never accept responsibility for your actions.

ONE
I didn't make us late!

TWO
That's denial.

ONE
That's not denial. I deny it!

TWO
You're digging yourself in deeper and deeper.

ONE
I got us here, to the door. We're here at the door and you won't go in.

TWO
And whose fault is that?

ONE
Are your legs paralyzed?

TWO
I will not dignify that with—

ONE
Or are you afraid?

TWO
Me, afraid? Of what?

ONE
That you'll go up to the door and step up on the sill and they won't let you in.

TWO
You idiot: why is the door open if they won't let us in?

ONE
Why are you here if you won't go in?

TWO
The problem is you turn everything into an intellectual game. You never accept the reality of your situation.

ONE
I have lived with the realities of your actions ever since That Day.

TWO
My actions? It was you!

> *ONE jerks on the rope, forcing Two a step toward One.*

ONE
It was you, and you just don't want to admit it.

> *TWO jerks on the rope, forcing One a step toward Two.*

TWO
You just waltzed off and tried to pretend it wasn't your fault.

> *They continue to haul on the line alternatively, not looking at each other, until they are side by side.*

Andrew Wetmore

ONE
After That Day, we never had another family reunion.

TWO
You drove grandma to an early grave.

ONE
Look how the kids turned out.

TWO
All our plans ruined.

ONE
Economic downturn—

TWO
Global warming—

ONE
All because of what you did!

TWO
All because of what you said!

> *They turn toward each other and realize how close together they are. After a moment One reaches a hand up toward the rope on Two's head.*

ONE
If you would just let go and admit it...

> *Two backs away, playing out the rope until they are at maximum distance again, saying:*

TWO
Me? There's nothing for me to admit.

> *They face out again. Pause.*

ONE
I have a headache.

TWO
You have no one to blame but yourself: carrying on like that—

ONE
You will drive me mad with your chatter-chatter-chatter!

TWO
Oh, it's all about you, isn't it? Everything's about you, except whose fault it is.

> *Beat.*
> *One tugs slightly on the rope. Two tugs sharply back.*

TWO
Don't you even think about it.

> *Beat.*

ONE
It's getting late. Once they close the door I don't think it ever opens again.

TWO
(turning to One)
Look at us! Look what you've done. I'm not going in there like this.

ONE
I didn't do this.

TWO
Well, I sure didn't do it.

Andrew Wetmore

ONE
Listen: we've just got to forget about it.

TWO
It doesn't work that way.

ONE
I'm forgetting all about it. Not thinking of the past anymore. Living only in the present.

TWO
So what else is new?

> *One tugs at the loop on their head, but it won't budge.*

ONE
I've had this thing on so long it's worn a groove in my head.

TWO
Oh, so now it's the rope's fault.

ONE
That door is going to close any second.

TWO
You should have admitted it was your fault long before this.

ONE
Who cares whose fault it is? Let's just get rid of this thing.

TWO
"Who cares"? "Who cares"? If you had cared in the first place this never would have happened.

ONE
(angry)
All right: I'm sorry! Okay? It's all my fault and I'm very very very sorry, all right? Satisfied?

    Tugs at loop.

ONE
Why won't this budge?

TWO
Because that was not a sincere confession.

ONE
What are you, the confessions guru?

TWO
How could I forgive you if you can't even say you're sorry properly? Not that I would forgive you even then...

ONE
Je m'excuse, Scussi! Perdoname! Soooooooorrrrrrry.

    Beat.

TWO
For what?

ONE
What?

TWO
For what are you sorry? I want to hear the whole song, not just the liner notes.

    One is about to snap back at Two yet again, but suddenly

realizes that, yes, they are sorry.

ONE
I'm sorry for...whatever it was. Whatever I did that upset you. Whatever.

TWO
(icy)
You don't even remember.

ONE
Give me a hint.

TWO
I have been carrying the pain of this all these years, and you don't even remember.

ONE
Listen, no kidding: we are out of time. Just tell me what it was. I am sorry that I don't remember what it was, but just tell me what it was.

TWO
It was...it was...
(can't remember what it was)
I shouldn't have to remind you. That's unforgivable in itself.

ONE
Nothing is unforgivable.

TWO
It suits you to say that.

ONE
Listen—

TWO
I am not listening any more.

ONE
I am sorry for any pain I have caused you.

TWO
You have proved again that you are a heartless beast, and forgiving you would just encourage you.

ONE
I am sorry for my part in tying us up like this.

TWO
(hands over ears)
La la la la la la la.

ONE
I am sick inside that I have caused you to waste energy hating me and resenting me, and that I couldn't find a way to make it stop. I am very sorry. Would you please forgive me?

TWO
If you think I am going to lay aside the grievances of my whole adult life because of a pretty speech—

> *One notices that their loop has loosened.*

ONE
Hey: look at this!

TWO
I will not look at anything! You don't even have the decency to let me finish a sentence.

Andrew Wetmore

ONE
And I know you don't want to hear this, but I forgive you, too.

TWO
What??

ONE
I forgive you. For anything and everything. And I love you.

> *One is able to slip the loop off their head. They holds it in their hands, marvelling.*

TWO
That is really the last straw. You forgive me! If there was anything to get forgiven for, I wouldn't go to you for it if you were the last person on earth.

ONE
The door is really going to close. I don't want to go in without you.

TWO
Let that be on your conscience, too. I am totally blameless, and you are, by your own confession, completely at fault.

ONE
Yes...

TWO
I wouldn't go through that door with you now even if you carried me.

ONE
That's final?

TWO
I am not talking to you any more until you...apologize for

apologizing the way you did for...that thing you did on That Day.

ONE
But—

TWO
Not another word.

> *After a moment, One puts the free loop over an arm of the chair (or hooks it on whatever set piece has been provided).*

TWO
And stop fidgeting. You're going to saw the top of my head off.

ONE
But—

TWO
Not a word!

> *One exits L through the door, leaving Two hooked to the chair. Two does not notice that One has left.*

TWO
Since we can't get rid of this, we'll just have to bear it. And it's not too awfully bad if you just don't talk about it. Just ignore it. What can't be cured must be endured.

> *Long beat.*

TWO
I didn't want to go through that door anyway: who knows what unacceptable people would be in there?

FADE OUT
END

Andrew Wetmore

The Face Chords

Time
Now.

Setting
A community hall in Nova Scotia. There is a table with chairs around it. SR is a table with coffee cups. Upstage there is a stand for a projection screen, with its hook up about six feet, but the screen is not in place. Kitchen is OSR; main door is OSL.

Cast

Leah: 20s, local girl who never left.

Joe: 20s, local boy returned home.

Winston: 70s, one of the founders of the group.

The music

The melodies for the two song excerpts are available through several YouTube postings, such as:
Happy Wanderer:
https://www.youtube.com/watch?v=5GgJHe0bC34
Logdriver's Waltz:
https://www.youtube.com/watch?v=upsZZ2s3xv8

The Face Chords

A community hall.
LEAH ENTERS SR, carrying a coffee urn. It is heavy and the trolley shelf for it is high. She is about to set it on the trolley when JOE, 20s, sticks his head in from SL.

JOE
Um.

Leah turns around, still holding the urn. Beat.

LEAH
That's it? Just "um"?

JOE
Um...sorry. You need a hand with that?

LEAH
Nope.

She laboriously turns back to the trolley.

JOE
Where is everybody?

Laboriously, Leah turns around again.

LEAH
I unlock the hall. I turn on the heat. I make the coffee. I am not in charge of the people.

JOE
I just want to know are we in the right place.

LEAH
I am, anyhow.

> *She starts to turn again. He sprints across the hall to help her put the urn on the trolley.*

LEAH
Careful!

> *Joe is leaning against the tap and hot coffee drizzles onto his leg and crotch.*

JOE
Yow! Hot! Hot hot hot hot hot.

> *He dances away, slapping at his thigh, which is now soaked. Leah puts the urn on the trolley.*
>   *WINSTON, with a cane, ENTERS SL.*

LEAH
You want a hand with that?

JOE
No! You've done enough.

LEAH
You did it to yourself, cowboy.

WINSTON
I see you met Leah.

JOE
Look at my pants!

WINSTON
Leah, this is Jim.

JOE
Joe.

WINSTON
(moving toward the table)
Joe. My driver today. Just moved back from away.

LEAH
There's a washroom through there, Jim.

JOE
Joe.

LEAH
Paper towels. Lotion.

JOE
I'm fine.

LEAH
(exiting SR)
Jim's a nice name.

WINSTON
(inspecting the chairs)
All set up. Leah takes good care of us.

Andrew Wetmore

JOE
What "us"? There's just you.

ALDON ENTERS SL.

ALDON
Sorry I'm late. Tractor wouldn't start, and then I couldn't get it to stop.

WINSTON
The others will be here soon.

ALDON
Winston, how are you?

WINSTON
Aldon, I could tell you a long, sad story—

ALDON
About the others--
(noticing Joe)
Oh. Who's this, then?

WINSTON
My driver. Just started.

JOE
(explaining the stain)
Coffee.

ALDON
Yeah. Does that to me, too.
(to Winston)
About the others—

WINSTON
(sitting)
Leah should put out some more chairs.

JOE
I could help.
Leah ENTERS with a rolled banner.

LEAH
Yes, you're Jim-dandy at helping.

    She goes to the stand.

JOE
Lemme reach that for you.

LEAH
Because I've only been doing this since forever.

ALDON
We don't need more chairs, Winston.

WINSTON
They always show up in a rush at the last moment. Where's our banner?

    Joe hangs the banner and unfurls it. It is blank.

JOE
Not much of a banner.

    Leah tries to turn it. The hook is out of her reach.

LEAH
(to Joe)
Well?

> *He lifts her up so she can turn the banner, his face against her stomach. The banner reads "The FACE CHORDS / Music from the Wood Lot".*

WINSTON
Much better. Now we're ready.

JOE
(looking around her at the banner)
"The Face Chords"?

LEAH
You can set me down now, mister.

> *He does and she retreats to the coffee cart, fanning her face at Aldon.*

JOE
A face cord is just a pile of firewood.

WINSTON
He's been out west so he doesn't know. The Face Chords, Jim,—

JOE
Joe.

WINSTON
—is the sweetest singing group ever. More than 20 woodsmen joining their voices to sing about the life we lead among the trees. We give concerts and raise funds for good causes.

JOE
That's you guys?

WINSTON
Like The Men of the Deeps, but no coal dust.

LEAH
He's the director.

JOE
Cool. Where's the rest of you?

ALDON
That's what we have to talk about, Winston.

WINSTON
Oh, the life in the woods!
(singing)
"I love to go a-wandering, along the mountain track--"

ALDON
Winston—

WINSTON
"And as I go, I love to sing—"

ALDON
Winston!

WINSTON
"My knapsack on my back...Val de ri..." Come on!

Aldon reluctantly provides harmony. They actually sing pretty well.

WINSTON AND ALDON
"Val de ri, val de ra, val de ri,
val de ra-ha-ha-ha-ha-ha
Val de ri, val de ra, my knapsack on my baaaaaaaack."

Andrew Wetmore

JOE
Hey, that's pretty good.

WINSTON
"I wave my hat to all I meet—"

ALDON
Nobody else is coming!

WINSTON
...What?

ALDON
Nobody else is coming, Winston. Nobody else wants to come.

WINSTON
But why?

ALDON
Because what's the point? How many were at the last rehearsal?

WINSTON
Now, that was a rainy day—

ALDON
There's always an excuse.

WINSTON
And that Trevor had his car in the shop--

ALDON
How many?

LEAH
Four. You was four.

ALDON
I'm sorry, Winston. But the Face Chords are so few now we could fit in one of them Smart cars.

JOE
Where did everybody go?

ALDON
Some went west, like you.

LEAH
And some ain't so spry as Winston.

WINSTON
Thank you, my dear.

ALDON
But there's a bigger problem. We're woodlot owners, sawlog wranglers. But the woods is gone away. The big machines come through and chew everything up and haul it off as biomass, and there's not a sawlog for an honest man to find.

JOE
Why would they do that?

LEAH
For money. Just like why you went out west.

ALDON
Our grandparents, they left the smaller trees to grow up, let the woods be healthy. A man could make an honest living, year over year, selectively harvesting, without leaving home. Now...yeah, Jim had to go west.

JOE
Joe. But I'm back.

ALDON
There's fewer and fewer working inthe woods, so fewer and fewer to sing about that life.

WINSTON
No more singing? No more Face Chords? But what am I going to do then?

JOE
I used to go in the woods with my uncle. We just cut a few cords for home, not to sell. But I loved doing that.

ALDON
Our way of life: the sea for fishing, the woods for logs and cord wood—

LEAH
And then the Legion for beer.

ALDON
If we worked an honest day, why not?

LEAH
It's not just you wood cutters that love the woods, eh. Not just you that loves the smells and the sounds and, oh yes, the warmth of a wood stove.

JOE
You're right. She's right. So you got to keep singing. To remind people we can't take the woods for granted.

ALDON
But where are the voices? Who will come listen to just one or two old fellas who can't carry a tune any more, much less a chain saw?

A pause. Then Leah begins to sing.

LEAH
"You can ask any girl in the parish around
What pleases her most, from her head to her toes—"

WINSTON
I never knew you could sing!

LEAH
Lots of things you don't know.
"She'll say I don't know that it's business of yours,
but I do like to waltz with a log driver."

WINSTON
Do I know that song?

LEAH
"For he goes burling, down, a-down the white water—"

JOE
What if...what if more than woodlot owners could join the group? Even women?

LEAH
Oh, thanks.

JOE
Sorry, but what if it was open to all people who love the woods? You'd find your voices.

ALDON
It's a better deal than just closing up shop.

WINSTON
You can't find singers just anywhere!

Andrew Wetmore

JOE
(singing)
"For he goes burling down, a-down the white water--"

He and Leah grin at each other.

ALDON
On the other hand, maybe you can.

LEAH AND JOE
(singing to each other)
"That's where the log driver learns to step lightly.
He's burling down, a-down the white water:
the log driver's waltz pleases girls completely."

ALDON
Winston, what do you say?

WINSTON
The boys will have to vote on it.

LEAH
They'll vote yes, if they ever want coffee again.
"At the end of the drive, I like to go down
and watch all the boys as they work on the river.
And when the day's over they'll be in the town,
and I do like to waltz with a log driver—

ALL
"For he goes burling down, a-down the white water,
That's where the log driver learns to step lightly.
He's burling down, a-down the white water:
the log driver's waltz pleases girls completely."

END

Consequences

Time
The day after an election.

Setting
A prison cell

Cast

Ana: Leader of the Loyal Opposition

Corporal: A man with dreams

Colonel: A servant of the nation

Andrew Wetmore

Consequences

A prison cell, somewhere, the day after an election. ANA is strapped to a chair L. She has been mistreated and is unconscious. A CORPORAL sits at a desk UC. On the desk are a thick file folder, a tin cup, and a baton or "persuader". A bucket with some water stands beside the desk.

The corporal consults his watch, gets up, strolls to Ana. He bends down to look at her. He takes her by the hair and brings her head upright. She remains unconscious, slack.

CORPORAL
Have you been a naughty girl?

He nods her head.

CORPORAL
Will you ever tell us what we want to know?

He shakes her head.

CORPORAL
Perhaps you need another lesson.

He nods her head.
The COLONEL ENTERS. The corporal does not see him.

CORPORAL
It will be soon, according to the schedule.

He moves her head back so her face is up toward his, and comes close to her as if they were going to kiss.

CORPORAL
Very...soon.

COLONEL
How is she today?

The corporal, startled, straightens up and turns. Ana's head lolls to one side.

CORPORAL
Sir. She is as she has always been, a foul pig of a traitor.

COLONEL
Until we detained her, she was a leader of the Institutional Reform Party: our loyal opposition.

CORPORAL
"Loyal". "Opposition". I understand each word separately, but put them together...?

COLONEL
She is an object of international attention. Especially now.

He crosses to the table.

COLONEL
Has she said anything more?

CORPORAL
Mainly gasps and grunts. But we have a good collection of compromising photographs now.

COLONEL
(examining a large photograph)
Is that you with her?

CORPORAL
The moustache is not enough of a disguise?

COLONEL
Oh, I'm sorry. I was not looking at the face.
(putting the photo back in the file)
You throw yourself into your work.

CORPORAL
Well...

COLONEL
What?

CORPORAL
I sometimes dream of a career in the cinema, sir.

COLONEL
You would leave this place?

CORPORAL
There are limits to how I can explore my creativity here. If someone dies under my care, do you know how many forms I have to fill out? Whereas out in the creative world I would have an agent to do all that.

COLONEL
You are well-informed.

CORPORAL
When they are unconscious, there is time to read and to dream. Perhaps our party, the great National Loyalty Party, needs publicity

movies...?

COLONEL
Wise artists hold on to their day jobs. Wake her up.

CORPORAL
Sir!

> *He goes to the table, takes the cup, scoops water out of the bucket, and approaches Ana.*

COLONEL
Gently!

CORPORAL
This *is* gently. Sir.

> *He dashes the water into her face. She splutters and starts to come awake.*

CORPORAL
"Not gently" is with the stick.

> *He returns the cup to the desk, makes a note in the file.*
> *Ana looks around as things come into focus. She stares at the Colonel.*

COLONEL
We meet again.

ANA
This is wrong.

CORPORAL
That's your opinion.

ANA
You don't come to me. I go to you. The room with the cigarettes. You let me smoke one, once.

COLONEL
Well, I am your good cop.
(to the Corporal)
Undo her.

CORPORAL
What?

ANA
What?

> *The Corporal hesitates. The Colonel starts toward her. The Corporal hurries forward, blocks his way.*

CORPORAL
Sir. I will do it, sir. In my holding cells, I am the one to bind and to let loose.

> *He undoes the straps from her arms and legs as the conversation continues. Ana massages her wrists slowly.*

COLONEL
You have been here for how long?

ANA
I...I don't know.

CORPORAL
Eleven weeks and three days.

COLONEL
Yes. Since the start of the electoral campaign.

ANA
It happened? The election?

COLONEL
Of course. And you voted: see?

> *Ana brings up her right hand. The index finger is stained purple.*

ANA
I don't remember voting.

COLONEL
Well, the excitement of the moment. A temporary amnesia.

ANA
Voting...
(to the Corporal)
More water?

CORPORAL
With pleasure.

> *The Corporal dips the cup in the bucket again, approaches Ana. She holds up a hand and he stops. She takes the cup of water from him and dashes it in her own face. Hands back the cup. The Corporal returns the cup to the table.*

ANA
You helped me vote, right?

CORPORAL
You would not have wanted to miss it.

ANA
You helped me vote for my party? For the Institutional Reform Party?

CORPORAL
No, as it turned out you voted for the People's Party.

COLONEL
(surprised)
The People's Party?

ANA
But—they want to overthrow everything—

COLONEL
—everything we hold dear—

ANA
—and let the common people lead.

CORPORAL
You always said you would die rather than vote for the People's Party. I wanted to see if it was true.

COLONEL
To make her vote for the People's Party...that was monstrously cruel.

CORPORAL
Thank you.

ANA
But now I die anyway.

CORPORAL
I did not see that memo.

ANA
What else could it be? The election is over and you have made it a

farce, despite the street protests, despite the UN observers, despite Jimmy Carter.

COLONEL
Mr. Carter was not allowed in the country.

ANA
And now the National Loyalty Party can claim a mandate.
(Standing with difficulty)
A mandate from the ballot box for further repression, further corruption. What was the result? 95% for National Loyalty?

COLONEL
It was not 95%.

ANA
So you were smarter than that.

COLONEL
Not exactly.

CORPORAL
(to Ana)
You see? You're wrong again!
(to the Colonel)
What?

COLONEL
It is harder than it used to be to get the results to come out as you want.

CORPORAL
What is so hard? You pick a number, you announce it.

COLONEL
Under international scrutiny...

CORPORAL
The observers can't be everywhere!

COLONEL
Robot drones with heat sensors, the exit polls, the likelihood algorithms, the microchips embedded in each ballot...At some point, without our realizing it, we moved into the future. And we were not ready for it.

ANA
What was the result?

COLONEL
It was not even close...

Ana takes him by the lapels.

ANA
What was the result?!

The Corporal grabs her.

CORPORAL
Oh, no you don't!

COLONEL
Let her go! Let her go.

The Corporal releases her.

COLONEL
I should not have kept you in suspense.
(Removing his uniform coat)
The people have spoken. It is a new era, and new bottoms must ease into the seats of power. Your party has won.

ANA	CORPORAL
What?	Impossible!

The Colonel drapes his coat over Ana's shoulders.

COLONEL
Elections have consequences. It is your new era.

He puts his hat on her head.

COLONEL
The "ins" are now out, and you who have been "out" for so long are now in.

ANA
We won...

CORPORAL
It must be a mistake.

COLONEL
But at least the People's Party are still under our boot heels.

ANA
Where they belong.

COLONEL
A directive has arrived. We must turn this facility over to you. I suppose I am now your prisoner.

He hands her his baton.

ANA
I have dreamed of a day like this.

She hefts the baton.

COLONEL
It has been in my dreams, also. I have awoken shaking.

CORPORAL
She is now in charge?

COLONEL
There will always be prisons. And the party in power will have the keys. Which reminds me...

He hands Ana a set of keys.

ANA
I must...I should...I don't know what to do first.

COLONEL
Elections have consequences. Now you must govern, instead of sitting at your ease in that chair.

Ana looks at the chair; looks at the Colonel.

ANA
The chair needs an occupant.

COLONEL
I will try to tell you everything, I suppose.

He moves past the Corporal to the chair.

ANA
Yes: you must know some interesting things.

CORPORAL
Wait!

ANA
(to the Colonel)
Does he often speak without being spoken to?

COLONEL
More and more.

CORPORAL
There is another way! There does not always have to be one of you sweating in the chair and the other one smoking the cigarette. I should not always have to be administering the slap, the stick, the...well, you know.

ANA
I know.

CORPORAL
Why should we always toil under this stone ceiling, these dank walls? Is this all there will ever be?

COLONEL
What are you saying?

CORPORAL
Don't you dream of a garden? Of a a comfortable chair in a quiet room with a good book?
(to Ana)
Don't you dream of riding a horse along the edge of the sea?
(to both)
I am just a corporal, but I have dreams, as you know. You must have greater dreams. Why should we not—follow them?

ANA
You mean...just leave?

COLONEL
Abandon this prison?

CORPORAL
Let all go out to their dreams who wish! Make a bonfire of the records...break up the devices of torture...change the whole story!

ANA
No revenge for what has passed? No exercising our new powers?

COLONEL
No hope for the next election?

CORPORAL
Elections can have wonderful consequences!

COLONEL
I have heard something like this crazy thing.

CORPORAL
(brandishing a pamphlet)
I was bored, and there was this flyer from the People's Party.

ANA	COLONEL
The People's Party?	The People's Party?

CORPORAL
It has some exciting ideas—

> *Ana drives the baton into the Corporal's stomach. He doubles over, falls backwards into the chair. The Colonel starts to strap him into place.*

ANA
We have no mandate to change the whole social order.

COLONEL
This is the better way. A government in office, yours or mine. A prisoner in the chair...

ANA
The institutions of state must endure, for the good of the people. Well, get on with it.

> *The Colonel pulls back the Corporal's head so they are looking into each other's eyes.*

COLONEL
So...have you been a naughty boy?

BLACKOUT
END

Customer Service

Time
A little bit into the future

Setting
A show room. There is a service counter and some bright, vague posters saying NEW! and JUST IN!
There is a display of brochures. Beside the counter there is a small step stool. There are products on shelves and on a sales rack. On the counter is a remote control device.

Note: the plays works best if the products and posters are notional or invisible, rather than the actual things one might find in such a shop. Far better (and less expensive) to leave it to the viewer's imagination.

Cast

Mr Johnson: the shop owner

Ben: a man in his twenties

Natalie: his partner, around the same age

Vicky: a pleasing woman, forever young

Andrew Wetmore

Customer Service

A show room. MR JOHNSON stands at the counter, doing some paperwork.
   BEN and NATALIE enter, look around at the decor.

BEN
They've changed since the last time we were in here.

NATALIE
Now we won't be able to find anything.

BEN
Spiffed it right up. Maybe they got a new owner.

NATALIE
I hope so. The last guy had a...look.

BEN
I didn't notice.

NATALIE
You were busy smelling the new-leather smell.

BEN
I love that smell.

JOHNSON
There's an app for that now.

BEN
There is?

JOHNSON
Right in your phone. Five leather types, from biker to sports car to cowboy. Creaking sound effects, too. How are you folks today?

BEN
Doing great.

NATALIE
We're just looking.

JOHNSON
Sale rack is over there.

>   *Natalie goes to the sale rack.*

BEN
Great...Actually, we're sort of looking for a new position.

JOHNSON
This would be for around the home, or for formal entertaining?

BEN
Not formal, no.

NATALIE
(looking at the items on the rack)
Got it...got it...too bright...I would never make *that* fit.

JOHNSON
We have some great new numbers for casual entertaining and

double dates.

NATALIE
Double dates?

JOHNSON
Certified up to 950 pounds.

NATALIE
We would never need that!

BEN
What if we had the Harrisons again? He's pretty hefty...

NATALIE
Oh. I suppose...oh, yes.

BEN
I guess we were mainly thinking of something for us, for around the house. We have a beater that just stopped working.

JOHNSON
Oh?

BEN
Well, I got bursitis here, so I can't really follow through the way I should.

JOHNSON
There's an app for that now.

NATALIE
But it's not the same. It's not the same.

BEN
No...So, we are just starting to think of picking up another position, give ourselves some options.

JOHNSON
Excellent idea. How many do you have at the moment?

NATALIE
Three.

BEN
We have more than three.

NATALIE
We have three. And forget about the beater now, so it's really just two.

BEN
What about the one we made up?

JOHNSON
You made one up? All by yourselves? That was daring.

BEN
It just came to me.

NATALIE
Not to me, though.

BEN
The second time it did.

JOHNSON
We carry a selection of locally-created artisan positions. You might consider marketing yours.

BEN
It doesn't even have a name, yet.

JOHNSON
Please to demonstrate.

NATALIE
Now?

JOHNSON
I am very curious.

BEN
Well, she puts her left foot on my right hip, and her hands—honey, hold the edge of your skirt in your teeth, remember?

NATALIE
Ben.

BEN
What?

NATALIE
No offence, Mr...

JOHNSON
Johnson.

NATALIE
Johnson, but what if we're on to something? We don't want to just give it away for nothing.

BEN
You're right. She's right. Besides, we need to work on it a bit more, fine-tune it.

JOHNSON
Of course. Try it out among friends, or with a focus group. But here is my card: when you are ready, we really should talk.

BEN
(taking the card)
Okay. Thanks.

JOHNSON
So that leaves us with two current positions. Well! On the bright side, it gives you room to expand.

NATALIE
All I want—

BEN
(looking at a poster)
Oh, that one's interesting.

JOHNSON
Just came in. Highly recommended for hot tubs, fresh-water frolics, and the like.

BEN
Looks sort of complicated.

NATALIE
I want something we can use, I don't know, on the kitchen counter, in the back seat of the car, in the hay loft...

JOHNSON
You have a barn?

NATALIE
I have a fantasy.

BEN
Is there, like, a brochure or a manual for this?

JOHNSON
Of course.
(calling)
Vicky? Could you join us, please?

> VICKY, the shop assistant, enters. She is wearing heels, a lab smock, plastic gloves, and not much else.

VICKY
Mr Johnson?

JOHNSON
This is Vicky. She is our manual for that position, and several others. She is certified for two-, three-, and four-person positions, and is a trainer for solo work.

VICKY
Hello.
(to Natalie, with interest)
Hello.
(taking the gloves off)
Oh, sorry. I was getting ready for a class.

JOHNSON
Vicky, this gentleman is interested in The Whirlpool.

VICKY
Oh, my.

BEN
But it seems a bit complicated...

VICKY
The main thing is to try not to breathe when your head is underwater. You have to time your breathing with your arm movements.

BEN
Oh, yes.

VICKY
You understand that this is not a position recommended for everyone. There are risks.

JOHNSON
Now, Vicky—

VICKY
And it requires a certain fitness level.

BEN
I work out.

JOHNSON
I am sure our friend—

BEN
Ben.

JOHNSON
—our friend Ben could master this position very quickly.

VICKY
(to Natalie)
May I check his hydraulics?

BEN
Yes, please.

NATALIE
I don't think that position is for us. But go ahead.

> *Vicky takes the step stool and comes close to Ben.*

JOHNSON
Good idea, Vicky. To get the best pressure, and therefore the best pleasure, a hydraulic rating of six or higher is important.

VICKY
Hi, Ben.

BEN
Hi...

> *Vicky slips her hand inside his shirt, runs it lightly over his chest. Draws her hand out and runs it over her own face.*

VICKY
You feel good. Smell good.

> *She puts the step stool down in front of him, quite close, and steps up on it. Draws him close so they are touching, body to body. She places her hands on his butt.*

VICKY
You said you work out?

BEN
I do. When I can.

VICKY
That can give you great glutes. Could you...clench for me? Ooh, that's nice. Again, please?

She kisses him, then steps down and returns the step stool to its place. Ben eases his trousers, which have suddenly become tight.

VICKY
His hydraulics seem just fine. Just fine. However, I don't think—

JOHNSON
Thank you, Vicky.

VICKY
But—

JOHNSON
Thank you.
(to Ben)
So, what do you think?

BEN
Oh, man.

NATALIE
Ben, he means what do you think of the position.

BEN
Oh.

JOHNSON
I'm sure we could knock a little bit off the price.

He flashes a brochure at Ben, who starts to read it.

NATALIE
But I wanted something simpler.

BEN
Just a second, dear.

JOHNSON
Vicky...

>   *He gives her a 'get going' gesture.*

VICKY
(to Natalie)
We can find you something simple, but exciting.

NATALIE
Yes?

VICKY
The sex position version of the little black dress.

NATALIE
That's what I want!

VICKY
Of course, with pearls costs a little more. But it can be amazing...

NATALIE
Pearls with...the dress?

VICKY
Pearls with...the position I want to show you.

>   *They look into each other's eyes.*

NATALIE
I never used pearls...

VICKY
The only thing is, make sure they're on a strong chain.

NATALIE
Chain.

VICKY
More fun than that Cirque de Soleil thing he's trying to sell you.

NATALIE
But why is he trying so hard with that?

VICKY
Bigger commission.

She moves Natalie a little further away. Johnson notices.

VICKY
You think he has your interests at heart—your sighing, your stretching, your exploding in ecstasy.

NATALIE
But no?

VICKY
No. He always wants you to be a little dissatisfied, a little incomplete, so you come back for another position, and another, and another—

JOHNSON
Vicky?

VICKY
Yes Mr Johnson?

JOHNSON
I can handle our friends now, thank you.

VICKY
But--

JOHNSON
Those devices won't oil themselves, will they?

VICKY
No...

> *She starts to move toward the back room, then rushes back and grabs Natalie's hand.*

VICKY
Take me with you.

NATALIE
What?

VICKY
Let me go with you. You won't be sorry.

NATALIE
I can't—

VICKY
I've got to get out. He treats me like a slave—the hours, the demonstrations. Do it over and over again, with special attention to the slow learners...You seem so nice, you two. I could make it nice for both of you.

NATALIE
But—

> *Vicky starts tugging her toward the door. Johnson picks up the remote.*

VICKY
I know a hundred and seven positions.

NATALIE
You do?

VICKY
Quick quick quick—

JOHNSON
Oh no you don't.

> *He aims the remote at her, presses the button. Vicky freezes in place.*

VICKY
Oh no, oh no.

NATALIE
Can't you move?

VICKY
Quick, drag me out the door.

> *Johnson puts down the remote and crosses to the women. Ben picks up the remote curiously.*

JOHNSON
I'm so sorry. She is just a beta, and sometimes—

NATALIE
She's not human?

VICKY
I have thoughts! I have feelings! I know a hundred and seven positions!

JOHNSON
She's a floor model, that's all.

NATALIE
But I thought—

VICKY
We're all floor models to him. Anybody that isn't him doesn't count. And all he wants is the missionary position, over and over again.

BEN
Just missionary?

NATALIE
All the time?

VICKY
That's all he knows, for all his big talk.

JOHNSON
Shut up!

VICKY
Over and over again. Missionary, missionary, mi-mi-mi-missionary. It's disgusting.

> Ben pushes a button on the remote.

VICKY
Oh! Oh, yes, Ben. Push it again.

Andrew Wetmore

BEN
Which one is it?

VICKY
More—let Natalie push it.

> *Johnson takes the control.*

JOHNSON
Give me that!

> *He pushes buttons. Vicky moans, gyrates, purses her lips, tosses her hair...finally slumps and is quiet.*

JOHNSON
I've only had her a couple of weeks. I'm still learning her controls.

NATALIE
Ben, she asked me to take her with us.

BEN
She did?

NATALIE
She's desperate. And she knows a hundred and seven positions.

> *They look at each other, then look at Johnson.*

JOHNSON
Oh, no, I'm sorry. She's not for sale.

BEN
What will you take for her?

JOHNSON
I couldn't, you understand. Just a floor model.

NATALIE
I don't care.

JOHNSON
But you saw her—sometimes she acts wild. There's no telling what kinks are in her software.

> *Ben and Natalie look at Vicky, and then at each other. They turn to Johnson.*

BEN
How much?

NATALIE
How much?

Blackout

End

Andrew Wetmore

The Story Of

Responding to the story of the Prodigal Son in the Gospel of Luke 15:11-32

Time
Now

Setting
A conference room at a Hollywood production company

Cast

Brenda: a young assistant

Luke: an author

Brad: a producer

Annette: a production associate

Gregor: a script consultant

Andrew Wetmore

The Story Of

> *A conference room. BRENDA, and assistant, leads in LUKE, a writer.*

BRENDA
So, Luke: this is the take-a-meeting room they told me to bring you to.

LUKE
Thank you.

BRENDA
They won't be long. They're always a little late, but not too much.

LUKE
They're very busy?

BRENDA
It doesn't matter. If you arrive late it looks like you're important and busy anyhow. If they were going to be on time, they'd wait around the corner for five minutes.

LUKE
I'm on time.

BRENDA
Well, you must be not important. Just kidding.

Andrew Wetmore

LUKE
Do you tell this to every visiting writer?

BRENDA
No. I just figured it out myself, and I had to tell someone. Don't tell them I told you!

LUKE
Your secret is safe.

BRENDA
With a writer? Ha.

LUKE
A writer, not a tattletale.

BRENDA
So, you wrote a script?

LUKE
It's just a story, still.

BRENDA
Is it good?

LUKE
I think so. I don't really—

BRENDA
It must be good. They wouldn't bring you out here to take a meeting if it was no good. It's not just any Matthew, Mark, or John that can get in here to pitch a picture idea.

LUKE
I have a copy with me. You could read it—

BRENDA
I don't read.

LUKE
And tell me what you think.

BRENDA
I'm not supposed to think. I came out here to be an actress, but that didn't work out and things sort of went sideways. And I...couldn't go home. I was lucky they gave me this job. If you can call it a job. I'm just here to bring you to the meeting and fetch the coffee.

LUKE
I'd, uh, like you to have it, anyway.

He gives her a copy of the script.

BRENDA
Well, then:
(mimicking the way he spoke)
I'd, uh, like to have it.

LUKE
You are an actor!

BRENDA
When you're famous I'll do you in my stand-up routine. You realize I'm nothing, right? I can't do anything for you.

LUKE
Maybe you can. Can I practice on you?

BRENDA
Sorry?

LUKE
I'm sort of nervous, so maybe if—

BRENDA
Oh, I get it. Gimme your elevator pitch.

She pushes an imaginary elevator button.

BRENDA
So, what's your script about?

LUKE
Uh...

BRENDA
Second floor.

LUKE
Hang on.

BRENDA
Third floor. Dunno how tall this building is.

LUKE
This father has two sons. The younger son takes his share of the estate, cashes out, and goes off. He wastes the money on wine, women, and—

BRENDA
Fourth floor.

LUKE
Then he has nothing. And he comes to his senses—

BRENDA
Top floor.

LUKE
—and he decides to go home and apologize to his father and face the music.

>   *Beat.*

BRENDA
And what happens?

LUKE
And the father welcomes him back as if he came back from the dead.

BRENDA
That happens?

LUKE
It happens this time. And then! The older son is really upset, because he didn't get to go off and have fun. It's like the younger son is being rewarded for being bad.

BRENDA
What does the father say?

>   *Three people ENTER talking. They are BRAD, a producer, ANNETTE, his assistant, and GREGOR, a script consultant.*

BRAD
(to Annette)
If we can't get Affleck, we'll have to get what's his name.

ANNETTE
(to Gregor)
Get Affleck. I think he's at that awards thing.

Gregor starts to dial a phone.

BRENDA
This is my floor, I guess.

BRAD
No: Affleck will want top billing this time. Even above the title.

ANNETTE
Get Brad Pitt in New York.

Gregor starts dialing again.

BRAD
Why Brad Pitt?

ANNETTE
Shorter name to fit over the title.

BRAD
Good thinking.

ANNETTE
(to Brenda)
Who is that? Delivery boy?

BRENDA
This is Luke.

BRAD
Luke?

BRENDA
You're taking a meeting with him about his story.

BRAD
Gregor? Am I taking a meeting with a writer named Luke?

Gregor hauls out a different device, starts consulting it.

LUKE
I—

ANNETTE
Don't interrupt!

BRENDA
(quietly to Luke)
If they aren't taking a meeting with you, it would be wrong to talk to you.

LUKE
Really?

BRENDA
They don't talk to civilians. They don't even talk to me unless it's about do they have a meeting.

BRAD
(to Annette)
Well?

ANNETTE
(to Gregor)
Well?

GREGOR
(closing device)
Yes. Meeting you has.

Andrew Wetmore

BRAD
Luke!
(pumping Luke's hand)
I am honoured to meet you. Call me Brad.

LUKE
Brad.

BRAD
I've had a string of successes in this tinsel town—

ANNETTE
Remarkable successes.

BRAD
—but I can tell you right now that what we're going to do with your story is going to top them all.

ANNETTE
Blow you away!
(Shaking Luke's hand)
I loved your story.

BRAD
This is Annette—

ANNETTE
Loved it!

BRAD
My associate production assistant.

ANNETTE
And I wanted to tell you three of our A-list stars are just panting to play the love interest.

LUKE
Love interest?

GREGOR
(Shaking Luke's hand)
Luffly story. Just luffly.

BRAD
And this is Gregor, our rewrite man.

GREGOR
What you prefer, haff fight scene before hero leafs home, or after when returning?

LUKE
What fight scene?

GREGOR
Is always fight scene. It must to be.

LUKE
But—who's fighting whom?

BRAD
"Whom": I love this guy.

ANNETTE
Love it!

BRAD
"Whom" is exactly the question, Luke. Get the whoms right and you've got your movie.

ANNETTE
So profound.

BRAD
That's why we're taking this meeting. Is there coffee, or do we die of thirst?

BRENDA
Won't be a minute.

    Brenda EXITS.

BRAD
It's a super script, Luke—

GREGOR
Is story only.

BRAD
What I meant. Super story. Boffo at the box office.

GREGOR
I can see in mind's ear.

BRAD
But there are one or two little changes we need to make so we can roll this thing up into an Oscar-class property.

ANNETTE
A clarification or two.

GREGOR
Couple leetle holes.

BRAD
I see the storyboard just fine. Act 1 is "King Lear" meets "Big". The kid gets his money and goes to the big city.

GREGOR
So is fight now, with daddy?

BRAD
Just a minute, Gregor. Act 2: think "Boogie Nights" meets "The Social Network"—high velocity, bright lights, noise, not too much clothes.

ANNETTE
Just enough clothes for product placements.

BRAD
Hold that thought, Annette. Act 2b is very topical, with a market crash and the kid has to go to work on some demeaning job like teaching.

    Brenda ENTERS with cups and a carafe on a tray.

BRENDA
Here's the coffee.

BRAD
Cream? Sugar?

LUKE
No, I'm fine.

BRAD
He doesn't want coffee, for cryin' out loud. Why didn't we know that? Get the man some juice, a seltzer water.

LUKE
I don't need—

BRAD
Let's go, girl!

BRENDA
Right away.

> *She EXITS*

BRAD
So there's the horrors of poverty in Act 2b. Then Act 3, when the kid comes home and the father welcomes him...and this is where we get a little confused, Luke. Is this "Return of the Jedi" and the kids topples his repressive family regime and liberates the servants? Or is it "Sounder" and the kid comes home and relieves the burdens of his aging parents?

LUKE
I don't think it's either of—

BRAD
You may be right. But remember, we've been in this business a lot of years, with a lot of successes. So work with us, okay?

GREGOR
If fight scene is in Act 3, we still leetle fight in Act 1 can have.

BRAD
Now there's two problems, and Gregor has put his thumb on one. In the fight scene—

LUKE
Do we have to have—?

BRAD
Oh, there's a fight scene. But who are the fighters? Who's slugging it out? The father and the kid? The two brothers? The old man and the older brother?

ANNETTE
That could be good. Your Bruce Willis types are very affordable, the older they get.

BRAD
In classical terms, we got to have a protagonist and a, and a—

GREGOR
Contagonist.

BRAD
And one of them has to win. And it has to be a win that makes us say "yes!" and feel ennobled and uplifted, and buy the action figure.

LUKE
The story isn't about people fighting—

BRAD
It's about people, isn't it? They fight and they screw, and we've got screwing covered in Act 1.

LUKE
Fighting isn't the only way to solve things.

GREGOR
Only good way.

ANNETTE
You have a person giving you trouble, you punch him or you shoot him—problem solved!

GREGOR
One guy—this.
(hands triumphantly in the air)
Other guy in pool of blood. Audience love.

BRAD
The combat question, Luke, is tied to the other problem: who is the story really about? Is it the story of the young man coming back to make things right?

ANNETTE
That guy from "The Queen's Gambit"!

GREGOR
Robert Downey, Jr. Can play anything.

BRAD
Or is it the story of the grumpy older brother?

ANNETTE
Oh, if we changed it to an older sister, maybe Meryl would do it.

BRAD
Or is it about the father who has to make a choice?

GREGOR
Eastwood!

ANNETTE
Redford!

BRAD
So we have to know who is it really about, before we can get on to casting and building publicity and, oh yes, a script.

LUKE
It's about all of them.

ANNETTE
A buddy movie?

GREGOR
Redford and Streep? Too expensive.

LUKE
What if everybody wins?

BRAD
I don't do fairy stories. But now that you've said that, Luke, it leads me to the last problem. This is a super story, no doubt about it.

GREGOR
Much hot.

ANNETTE
Perfect in every way.

BRAD
Except it doesn't have an ending yet. The kid comes home, the father welcomes him—big surprise. Then the big brother is all upset—bigger surprise. Then dad tells the big brother, don't be such a noodge...

ANNETTE
And then?

GREGOR
And then?

BRAD
And then we don't know what happens. What do the brothers do?

GREGOR
Now is fight?

ANNETTE
Who gets the girl?

BRAD
We don't want the audience to have to try to figure it out.

GREGOR
Oh, no.

ANNETTE
No, no.

GREGOR
(looking at PDA)
Hey, boss. You got other meeting.

BRAD
When?

GREGOR
Five ago minutes.

BRAD
Perfect.

> He shakes Luke's hand.

BRAD
So there it is, Luke. Nobody ends a movie with a question.

> Brenda ENTERS with a tray of non-coffee options.

BRAD
Give it some thought, then pitch us the ending. Have your person call my people.

> Brad EXITS.

ANNETTE
(shaking hands)
Here's a thought to run with: what if the love interest fights with the daughter? If the older brother is a sister. We'll be in touch.

Annette EXITS

GREGOR
Good story. And don't worry: I will help with rewritings.

Gregor EXITS.
Beat.

BRENDA
I brought your juice.

LUKE
Oh. Thanks!

BRENDA
I would have been here quicker, but I was reading your story.

LUKE
You don't read.

BRENDA
I'm thinking maybe I should. I liked your story. I know they all said they loved it, but they have to say that. To your face, anyway. But I really liked it.

LUKE
Thanks.

BRENDA
I like the way it ends. With a question? It made me, sort of, you know...

LUKE
Think?

BRENDA
That's the one. Yes.

> *Beat.*

BRENDA
Well. I guess I'll take you back to reception now.

LUKE
I guess I'll see you at the next meeting.

BRENDA
Oh. Maybe not. After I read your story, I started thinking maybe I should go back home for a while. See my folks. Sort some things out.

LUKE
Can these guys get their own coffee and juice?

BRENDA
They'll have to learn, won't they. Terrible tough. This way, Mr Story-teller.

> *They EXIT.*

BLACKOUT
END

Big Wheel

Time
The present

Setting
A Ferris wheel in an amusement park, late in the evening. The wheel arcs up out of our view; we can see one car on the upward curve (SL), and one on the downward (SR).

Production note: we can trust the audience's imagination and use a minimal set, Thornton Wilder-style. The wheel can be entirely notional, and the two cars two pairs of rocking chairs tied together. Depending on your performance space, you may need to rig a low structure to allow Sherm to appear from below the level of the cars.

Cast

Des: a retired businessman, in his 60s

Doph: Des's wife, in her 60s

Bill: a rising entrepreneur, 40s

Anik: Bill's companion, 20s

Sherm: a maintenance man, 40s

Andrew Wetmore

Big Wheel

A Ferris wheel. The two cars we can see each hold a couple: SR are DES and DOPH. SL are BILL and ANIK. Halfway between the cars is a box or contraption representing the centre of the wheel.

   The cars are not moving on their cycle, but Anik is making their car rock back and forth.

ANIK
Come on come on come on!

BILL
Stop it, Anik.

ANIK
Make it go.

BILL
It will go real soon.

ANIK
You promised you would take me to the top.

BILL
And I will.

   She stops agitating the car.

BILL
Modern Ferris wheels are really hi-tech. If something goes a little bit wrong, they stop real quick until it can get fixed.

ANIK
When it stopped so real quick, I lost a shoe.

BILL
I'll get you another. I'll get you a dozen.

ANIK
I wanted that one.

BILL
Who wants just one shoe? Here...

> *He take the foot that still has a shoe on it, ifts the leg, and starts to run his other hand slowly up it.*

ANIK
Bill! Not here.

BILL
Where, higher?

ANIK
Stop: don't you ever think of anything else?

BILL
Of course I do.

> *He slips off her remaining shoe, lowers her leg, and releases her.*

BILL
For example, right now I was thinking of keeping you balanced.

ANIK
So now I have no shoe.

BILL
See? Balanced.

ANIK
I don't want balanced. I want up.

> *They look out over the vista. Bill looks up toward the top of the Ferris wheel.*

ANIK
We are still not moving.

BILL
Just enjoy the view, okay? We'll be moving again soon.

ANIK
With no shoes.

> *They look around.*

BILL
Amazing. We were down there once.

ANIK
They are so far away.

BILL
Like ants. Just ants. If you had shoes you could squish 'em, ha ha.

ANIK
Why would I do that?

BILL
Because that's what you do to ants.

DOPH
(to Des)
So crass.

DES
Eh?

DOPH
So crass. Over there.

Des starts to look at Bill

DOPH
Don't stare at him.

DES
I'll stare at whoever I want to stare at.
(to Bill)
Hello, there.

BILL
Hello.

DES
All right over there? You don't mind trailing behind?

ANIK
We are not moving.

DES
I know we are not moving, my dear.

ANIK
But why are we not moving?

BILL
I know you.

DES
Lotta people know me.

BILL
I heard you speak at that seminar on success. You were great!

DES
Did you?
(to Doph)
He heard me at a seminar. And I was great.

DOPH
He's blocking my view.

DES
He's what?

DOPH
He's blocking my view. Over there. I liked that view when we were on the way up.

DES
Woman, you're as blind as a bat. What do you need a view for?

DOPH
You called it "our view". Back when we first saw it.

DES
All right, all right. Look over this way: this is "our view" now.

DOPH
(looking)
It's not the same.

BILL
Yeah, you did some great things. I'm Bill, by the way.

DES
I did, yes.

BILL
And this is Anik.

DES
Your daughter?

BILL
(laughing)
Oh, no. No no. Not daughterly at all.

DOPH
I told you. Crass.

DES
My God, she looks about eleven. And she's all legs.

ANIK
(to Des)
How can we make the car move?

BILL
Just wait.

ANIK
I want to go.

DES
I wouldn't hurry, miss. Look up. The very top is not that far away.

ANIK
(looking)
What are they doing up there?

DES
They have an even better view.

DOPH
And nobody can block it.

DES
We used to have that view. You can see three counties from there.

BILL
I heard that.

DOPH
Can hardly see a sewer district from here.

DES
Look somewhere else. Look at Anik.

DOPH
(to Anik)
Hello, dear. I am Doph, and this is Des.
(to Des)
They are made for each other, despite her legs.

ANIK
What is wrong with my legs?

DOPH
Excuse me: I was speaking to my husband.

ANIK
There is nothing wrong with my legs. I compare them to your legs any day.

> *She stands up, hikes up her skirt to display her legs. The car wobbles.*

BILL
Woah!

DOPH
Sit down.

ANIK
I stand if I want. I dance if I want. And we are going to the top!

DOPH
Yes? Well, we have been to the top. I am not at all sure I would want to go back.

DES
What?

DOPH
I would have been happier with my view.
(Shifts in her seat)
And a slightly thicker cushion.

DES
You crazy coot, I'd go back in a heartbeat. It was the best.

BILL
Good times up there, huh?

DES
Oh, sure, parties and all that. But the view...the vision you have from the top...you can't beat that.

ANIK
There are parties?

DOPH
Not the sort of party I imagine you are used to. We kept our clothes on, for one thing.

DES
(laughing)
Most of the time.

DOPH
You're as crass as they are.

DES
Crass my ass. You loved it.

DOPH
Not to discuss with just anyone.

ANIK
When the wheel starts again, and this car starts to rise, rise, toward the top, what happens to your car then, I wonder?

BILL
Anik—

ANIK
She started it. I just finish it.

> *Anik sits down.*

BILL
(to the others)
She doesn't mean anything.

> *Anik kicks at him.*

ANIK
Don't you say that about me. I always mean something.

BILL
Yes. Yes, you do.

DES
(to Doph)
Caught a wildcat.

DOPH
Told you.

> *There is a CLANGING sound from below.*

ANIK
What was that?

BILL
It's nothing.

ANIK
Will we fall?

BILL
Come on. If we were going to fall, it would be a much bigger sound.

> *There is a much bigger CLANG.*

DES
(looking down)
There he comes.

DOPH
I bet you five cents he calls me "dearie".

DES
(calling down) Need a hand?

SHERM
(from below)
Yeah: gimme a hand.

> *Doph and Des start applauding.*

DES
(to Bill)
The old jokes are the best, you know.

BILL
Who is that?

DES
Why, that's Sherm! Most important guy on the whole big wheel.

ANIK
He owns this wheel?

DES
Better than that. He makes it run, and he fixes it when it stops.

ANIK
(calling down)
Hello, Sherm! I am Anik.

> *SHERM starts to climb into site. He has overalls and a tool belt.*

BILL
(to Anik)
Sit down: you'll fall.

ANIK
I never fall.

SHERM
Only takes once. Sit down, miss—

ANIK
Anik.

SHERM
Sit down, Anik, okay?

ANIK
You will make the wheel go?

DES
He never fails.

DOPH
It only takes once.

ANIK
Don't listen to her, Sherm. She is just a ghost-woman over there. Just waiting for the ride to be over.

SHERM
Simmer down, now. Lemme look at this.

Sherm is now in between the two cars, studying some mechanism.

BILL
(calling upwards)
Hello! Hi, up there! Sherm is fixing things. We'll be moving soon.

DES
They don't want to hear that. And they don't want to hear it from you. Tell them they will be there forever: they would like that.

SHERM
(to himself)
One of these days, this damn thing will just—freeze.

ANIK
It will?

SHERM
What?

ANIK
It will just freeze?

SHERM
I was just talking to myself.

BILL
Don't bother the man.

ANIK
(to Bill)
Can you make the wheel turn? No? So why should I listen to you?

BILL
Because—because we are going to the top together.

ANIK
Do you think?

BILL
Of course we are. I promised.

ANIK
And then what?

BILL
Then...we will be at the top.

ANIK
And then what, Bill? Ask Des. Des, what happens then?

DES
Don't spoil his ride.

DOPH
You know what happens. He knows, too.

ANIK
Even the ghost woman knows. Then we go down. Right? Right?

BILL
Right now we are going up. let's concentrate on that part.

ANIK
But we are not going up. We are just hanging here. You cannot make us go up.

BILL
None of us can make the wheel move before its time.

DES
There's wisdom for you.

ANIK
Sherm can make it move.

DOPH
Not doing too good of a job right now.

SHERM
(fiddling with the machinery)
That dang thing is just about stripped.

ANIK
Let me help.

>   *She starts to climb out of the car.*

BILL
What are you doing?

ANIK
Don't touch me!

BILL
Stop!

>   *Anik edges toward Sherm.*

ANIK
I can help you hold that.

SHERM
You ever work on one of these?

ANIK
You can teach me.

SHERM
Get back in the car.

ANIK
I must ask you a thing. When the wheel turns, the people go down and down, and then they are at the bottom, and then they are gone, yes?

BILL
Anik!

SHERM
Yes. That's how it is.

ANIK
But you are not gone.

SHERM
Oh, no. I'm up and down this thing all day long.

ANIK
You even can climb right up to the top, yes?

SHERM
(uneasy)
I could, yes.

ANIK
And you have, I bet. When everyone is gone, you climb up into the very top and the whole wheel is yours. Just yours.

SHERM
Maybe.

DES
Sherm! You haven't even paid for the ride.

SHERM
Without me, there is no ride.

ANIK
(to Bill)
Without him there is no ride.

DOPH
Oh, get on with it, Sherm. I am tired of hanging here over nothing.

DES
I'm not.

ANIK
(to Sherm)
I could help you.

BILL
Anik—

ANIK
I can be helpful in many ways. Ask Bill how I help him.

BILL
Come back.

ANIK
If I am your helper...

SHERM
Yes...?

ANIK
Could I climb with you to the top? You could show me the top.

SHERM
You have to climb down, too. Up and down this old thing all day long.

ANIK
I could do that. With you.

DOPH
Crass upon crass.

DES
Take her, man! She'll keep you warm on winter nights.

SHERM
Well, you're very presentable, and you have nice, long legs.

ANIK
Strong legs: feel.

SHERM
But, heck, it won't do. You don't have shoes.

ANIK
But—

SHERM
Climbing up and down, up and down. You would rip your feet to shreds in an afternoon.

ANIK
(to Bill)
I hate you! Without you I would still have shoes.

BILL
Without me you wouldn't be here at all.

SHERM
(of the machinery)
Well, that about does it. You get back in your car, miss. I'm going to climb down and see will she run now.

ANIK
You don't want me?

SHERM
Well, sure. But not without shoes.

> *He starts to climb down; looks up at her.*

SHERM
Sure is a pity: nice long legs and all.

DOPH
A gentleman would not stare up her skirt.

SHERM
A gentleman couldn't fix this here wheel, dearie.

DES
(laughing)
You're done now, Doph. Not a thing you can say to that.

DOPH
Do you think so?

DES
Come on, now—

DOPH
You've known me all these years—

DES
Don't get involved. We're nearly done here.

DOPH
Good reason to get involved, I think.
(to Anik)
Here, crass girl. Take my shoes.

BILL
What?

ANIK
What?

DOPH
Come over here. Use my shoes.

ANIK
Why?

DOPH
Do you want to follow that crass man who likes looking up your skirt?

ANIK
(crossing to Doph's car)
If he gets me to the top, he can look at whatever he wants.

DOPH
Then take the shoes.

BILL
Anik, you don't know what you're doing! You'll fall!

ANIK
(putting on the shoes)
But I know what you're doing. You will rise to the top, maybe. And then you will fall again and be gone, for sure. And that will be all.

BILL
You'll fall right away.

ANIK
Not me. Look: I got sensible shoes!

>   *She moves to the centre.*

BILL
That's it. Keep coming!

>   *Anik starts to climb down the path Sherm took.*

BILL
(faintly)
No...

ANIK
Sherm! Sherm, look up!

>   *She waggles her butt.*

ANIK
Here I come to you!

>   *She is gone.*

DES
Well, you ditzy dame. Now you got no shoes.

Andrew Wetmore

BILL
She's gone.

DES
She was gone from you long ago, sonny.

BILL
What do you know, anyway.?

DES
Get this far, and you will know a lot. Understand a lot. Only thing I never understood
(of Doph)
was *her*.

DOPH
Now she isn't blocking my view.

DES
I told you, we got a perfectly good view over here.

DOPH
So now we have two.

DES
If I live to be a hundred...You want my shoes, you old dame?

DOPH
What would I do with shoes?

BILL
What could I do with a shoe?

DES
Eh?

Bill starts to get out of his car, studying the machinery. He has Anik's shoe.

BILL
I didn't really understand. I thought the point was to get up to the top. I never thought about after.

DES
They never tell you that part.

BILL
Do you like where you are? On the way down.

DES
I was getting tired, up there at the top.

DOPH
It is better than being down there.

DES
Well, yeah: because you got no damn shoes.

BILL
What if you could stay longer?

DES
Eh?

BILL
If the wheel never moves, you never have to go down.

DES
You never get to the top.

BILL
No. But this is already higher than I ever thought I would get.

DES
The key to success is believing in yourself. I read that in my book.

> *Bill is at the contraption in the centre. He jams the shoe into the gearing.*

BILL
Maybe that will jam the gears.

DOPH
Young man, do you really think that will work?

BILL
If it doesn't work, the worst thing for me is that I go up.

DES
Ha!

DOPH
While you wait...

BILL
Yes?

DOPH
Could you not block my view?

BILL
Oh! Sorry.

> *He climbs back into his car. They all look out at the view.*

SHERM
(below)
Going to crank 'er up now...

> *There is a GRINDING SOUND. Then a loud BANG.*

SHERM
(below)
What the hey—?

ANIK
(below)
You said you could make it run!

SHERM
(below)
Don't you start, now!

BILL
(to himself)
And perhaps Anik will climb up to see what's wrong...

DES
(to Doph)
Not so dumb, after all.

DOPH
Did I ever say he was dumb?

> *She puts her feet in Des's lap.*

DOPH
Here: rub my feet. That will make it just perfect. For as long as it lasts.

FADE OUT
END

Andrew Wetmore

An Earthly Nurse

Time
Summer

Setting
A beach

Cast

Sue: A young nurse with a passion

Doug: A business man on the beach

Andrew Wetmore

An Earthly Nurse

> *In the blackout, the SOUND of a SEAL.*
> *At lights up, a beach. SUE, a young woman in a bathing suit is scanning the water. Nearby, a blanket, some clothes, and a basket lie on the sand.*

SUE
Where are you? Why don't you just show yourself? I want to swim with you.

> *DOUG enters L. He has a metal detector with its earphones on, but otherwise he is fairly presentable.*

SUE
Come on! I'm not kidding!! I can't wait forever.

> *Doug takes his earphones off, switches off the detector.*

SUE
I need you to come back right now. It matters to me!

> *She looks around, sees Doug.*

SUE
Oh!

DOUG
Child or dog?

SUE
What?

DOUG
There's a big collie a ways up the beach.

SUE
No. No, that's not him.

DOUG
But it isn't a child that wandered off.

SUE
No—oh, no. He's quite grown up.

DOUG
One of those terrier breeds? They're always taking off after rabbits, or flapping bits of newspaper, or an errant thought.

> *They look at each other. Sue suddenly feels exposed and puts on a long t-shirt over her bathing suit.*

SUE
Are you a dog person?

DOUG
I tried once. It ran away as soon as it could. Seemed cruel to try again. Name?

SUE
(startled)
Uh, Sue.

DOUG
All right.

Andrew Wetmore

(yelling)
Sue! Suuuuuue!! Come on, Sue! Nice puppy biscuit for you here. Nice ride in the car with your head out the window.
(looking around)
Maybe he doesn't come for strangers.

SUE
He does quite well once the first awkward moments are past.

DOUG
Pound puppy?

SUE
He found me on this beach, just over there. I think he had travelled a long way. He was shaking, but so beautiful. Glossy.

DOUG
Sue! Sue!!

SUE
(amused)
That won't bring him.

DOUG
Oh? Do you have some enticing way of calling 'Sue' so he feels sleek and comfortable and greatly loved?

SUE
That's my name. Not his.

DOUG
It is?

SUE
When you said, 'Name?' like a border guard, I thought you meant, well, me.

DOUG
Typical. I'm Doug. Tough name to say so the hearer feels all sleek and loved and, um...

SUE
I think it could be done.

> *They gaze at each other.*

DOUG
So. What name do we call to get his attention?

SUE
Oh. Well. I...he responds to my voice, I don't have to use any special words.

> *They look at each other.*

DOUG
Well. I guess I should—

SUE
What do you find with that thing?

DOUG
With this? Mainly pull-tabs off beer cans. I've never worked this beach before—

SUE
No. I mean, I've never seen you, and I'm here a lot.

DOUG
I was working up the coast a ways. I found a guy's wedding ring once.

SUE
Wow!

DOUG
But it was still attached to the guy, or what was left of him.

SUE
What did you do?

DOUG
Called the cops. The widow seemed strangely pissed that I had found the body, and she had a lot of biker friends. So I thought I would try another beach.

SUE
Are you...? Is this what you—?

DOUG
Oh, no. I have a respectable job in an office.

SUE
With no dress code.

DOUG
No. Well, to tell you the truth, I can't go there right now.

SUE
Laid off?

DOUG
My lawyer says I should stay away until...well, just "until".

SUE
What did you do?

DOUG
Nothing.

SUE
Who did you do it with?

DOUG
No. No, nothing like that.

SUE
That's what they all say.

DOUG
I wouldn't know.

> *He puts his earphones back on, turns his back to her, starts scanning the sand again.*

SUE
I'm sorry.

DOUG
Can't hear you.

SUE
Yes, you can!

> *Doug stops scanning the sand. Shuts off the machine. Stands dejected.*

DOUG
Might as well just walk into the ocean.

SUE
The people I work for get crabby when I want to take time off.

DOUG
What do you do?

> *He takes his earphones off.*

SUE
I'm just a nurse. Part of a team for this rich lady who could get better care in a nursing home than in her own house, but there you are.

DOUG
You must have regular time off.

SUE
So I stretch it a bit sometimes....But it's crazy. The bedpan, the intravenous: as long as one is empty and the other is full, why should they care?

DOUG
The place where I work, I started it with some other guys. We saw a need, built a product, and it's going okay. The other guys, they think it should be doing way better than that. They think we should all be crazy rich, right now. They want to do things I think are wrong.

SUE
"Wrong" like...that body you found?

DOUG
No, no. "Wrong" like cutting corners. Going for quick profits. We've been fighting about it and now they're trying to squeeze me out.

SUE
Can they do that?

DOUG
My lawyer says no. But he also says I am my own worst enemy, so I should keep out of the way for a few weeks.

SUE
What do your friends say?

DOUG
Those other guys I mentioned? Those were my friends.

SUE
Can you—?

DOUG
Forget those guys. It makes me itch to think about them. So you're a beach person.

SUE
Never was. But now...I'm here a lot.

DOUG
I'll help you find him.

SUE
Why?

DOUG
I'd like to help.

SUE
You don't even know me.

DOUG
I know you need help.

Andrew Wetmore

SUE
And I know what that means. When strange guys say, 'I'd love to help', they mean, 'I'd love to help myself.'

DOUG
Oh, please.

SUE
More guys hit on me than hit on you, I guess, so I think I know what I'm talking about.

DOUG
Every time I try to—
(collects himself)
Did you lose your dog or not?

SUE
I never said he was a dog.

DOUG
Your mongoose.

SUE
No.

DOUG
Your mind.

SUE
You will never, not in a million—

DOUG
Your seal.

SUE
What?

DOUG
Your, you know, what's that thing in the legend, the seal that turns into a guy.

SUE
How— How did you—?

DOUG
A slurpie. A smoothie. Oh, a silkie!
(singing)
'An earthlie nourris sits and sings,
And aye she sings, ba-lillie-wean—'

SUE
There's a song?

DOUG
You never heard it?

SUE
He's mine. He's not public property for anybody to just sing about.

DOUG
If he was the guy in the song, he wouldn't be yours. You'd be his.
(singing)
'Little ken I my bairnis father,
Nor yet the land that he dwells in...'
(speaking)
There's like fifty verses.

SUE
What's a 'bairni'?

DOUG
Bairn. Baby.

SUE
Well, there's no baby, so forget it.

DOUG
(singing)
'Then one arose at her bed-feet,
And a grumly guest I'm sure was he—'

SUE
'Grumly' better mean sexy.

DOUG
(singing)
Saying, 'Here am I, thy bairnis father, Although that I be not comely.'

SUE
He is totally comely. If 'comely' is a good thing.

DOUG
(singing)
'I am a man upon the land,
I am a silkie in the sea—'

SUE
Party trick. You're making this up.

DOUG
Am not.

SUE
Or you've been watching us.

DOUG
Oh, come on.
(beat)

Wait, you're not kidding. You lost your guy—

SUE
I didn't lose him--

DOUG
—and he told you in his day job he's a seal.

SUE
He's due back. I've been waiting. Every few weeks he comes out of the sea here, so glossy and naked and mine.

DOUG
(scanning the ocean)
He just pops up? Like a cork?

SUE
The first time I was swimming. It was the end of the afternoon. There was a seal—every time I looked it was a little closer. And then it was gone and he was there, very close. Very close. We swam and basked and touched...

DOUG
What's his name?

SUE
He didn't say his name.

DOUG
Could he speak? Could he understand you?

SUE
Oh, he understood me.

DOUG
Wow. And this has happened more than once?

Andrew Wetmore

SUE
All the time. Well, three times. I come to the beach whenever I can, just in case. I wait and wait...

> *They look at each other*

SUE
What?

DOUG
You know there's a nude beach about three miles that way? I bet he's one of those grumly folkloric predatory naturists having you on.

SUE
If you saw him, you'd know.

DOUG
That's certainly true.

SUE
(singing tentatively)
'An earthly nourris...'
(speaking)
What's a 'nourris'?

DOUG
A nurse.

SUE
So you are making it up! I tell you I'm a nurse and you stick me in a song.

DOUG
First, the song was there before I was born. Second, would that be the worst thing anyone ever did for you?

SUE
...Nobody ever put me in a song before.

DOUG
It's generally considered a nice thing. Not that I did it.

SUE
Then I don't have to say thank you.

    They look at each other.

DOUG
OK, then. I'll help you find your silkie.

SUE
Why?

DOUG
Nobody should be alone.

SUE
Are you? Alone?

DOUG
A little bit.

SUE
Sir, is that a shameless play for sympathy?

DOUG
Shameless.

    They look at each other.

SUE
How does that work?

DOUG
A shameless play for sympathy?

SUE
I know how *that* works. How does the detector thingy work?

DOUG
Do you want to try it?

SUE
I—

DOUG
Here...

> *He turns her so she is facing away from him, steps close behind her, and arranges the strap for the metal detector so it is over both of them.*

DOUG
You see that dial, there? When you swing the head over something it's sensitive to, that needle jumps up over there, and there's a buzzing sound.

SUE
You just...

DOUG
Put your hands there, and swing it slowly back and forth.

> *She does this for a couple of moments.*

SUE
There's no buzz.

DOUG
Well, it isn't on.

SUE
How do I turn it on?

> *She stops swinging the thing, stands thoughtfully against him.*

SUE
And yet...I am sensing something pretty big.

DOUG
Oh. That. Sorry.

> *She turns so she is still inside the strap, but now she is facing him as they stand pressed together.*

SUE
But sir, we've scarcely been introduced.

DOUG
Why stand on ceremony?

> *He leans toward her, she raises her head toward his. Then they move as far apart as the strap permits.*

SUE	DOUG
No.	No.

> *They lean in toward each other again.*

DOUG
Just a token of my esteem.

Andrew Wetmore

SUE
You build up a head of esteem pretty quick.

DOUG
You esteem me up.

SUE
This is crazy.

> *She puts her hand on his chest.*

SUE
I have my man already. Seal. Silkie.

> *She ducks out of the sling.*

SUE
And we're going to find him, right?

DOUG
That's the plan.

SUE
So...shouldn't I be, shouldn't I stay—

DOUG
Faithful?

SUE
That's not a bad word, you know.

DOUG
Do you think he is?

SUE
Faithful?

DOUG
Yeah. Like, where is he when he isn't here?

SUE
He's out being a seal, is where he is. Like in that song.

DOUG
You know they have girl seals, right?

SUE
Oh. They do.

DOUG
And the best boy seals have like harems of girl seals.

SUE
They do? They would.

DOUG
Think about it. If he's out there with all those slick, glossy girl-seals, but he's being faithful to that human girl on the beach, he wouldn't be a very good seal, would he? Not a credit to his species.

SUE
Are you? A credit to your—?

DOUG
Oh, yes.

SUE
Could you...step away a little bit? I need to think about this, and you...

She fans her face.

DOUG
Of course.

> *He steps downstage; she kneels among her stuff, buries her face in her towel.*

DOUG
A touch of sun, that's what it is. You should drink some water.

> *Doug notices something in the water behind the audience SR..*

SUE
I never met anyone like him.

DOUG
We could go find some shade; get a cool drink.

SUE
Everything else is so gray, so flat, beside him. Not you, of course, but I just met you.

DOUG
Not flat: I'm flattered.

> *He shoos angrily at something in the water, then checks if Sue is watching.*

DOUG
We should go search for your beast up the beach.

SUE
My…beast.

DOUG
(pointing SL)
Maybe that way.

SUE
I don't think he's coming.

Doug picks up a rock to throw at the thing he has seen.

SUE
I even brought a sort of a picnic.

DOUG
Smoked salmon?

SUE
Ha ha.
(gathering her things)
Would have been simpler...

DOUG
What?

SUE
If I could have met you six months ago.

DOUG
Six months ago I wasn't as nice.

SUE
You seem nice now.

DOUG
(deciding not to throw the rock)
A little.

SUE
(standing)
We're not going to find him.

DOUG
That's no way to—

SUE
You don't even believe he exists.

DOUG
I really do.

SUE
Well, I'm not sure any more. But if he is real, he'll have to find me. I don't have magic powers. I'm just a—what is it in the song?

DOUG
An earthly nourris.

SUE
A stupid, gullible nourris. But when he finds me—f he does—we are going to get some things clear right away.

DOUG
Good plan.

> She bundles her stuff in front of her. Doug scans the sea anxiously.

SUE
What did you find?

DOUG
Nothing.

He puts the rock in his pocket.

SUE
You picked something up.

Doug aims the detector at her, makes a beeping sound.

DOUG
Found a treasure. Way cooler than a wedding ring on a finger bone.

SUE
Aw, you're sweet-talkin' me again.

They step closer to each other. Doug turns her so she is facing L. She hugs him. He scans the sea over her head.

DOUG
Sue.

SUE
You called?

DOUG
Shall we go?

Sue steps back from him.

SUE
No.

DOUG
But—

SUE
Love at first sight with a seal may be...interesting. Falling for someone else after thirty seconds is totally not.

DOUG
I could overlook it.

SUE
(gesturing SL)
You're going that way?

DOUG
Yes...No! No, I'm going to go on up that way. Miles of detecting ahead of me.

SUE
All right. I'll go that way.

DOUG
And that's that?

SUE
I don't know.

DOUG
Will you be here again?

SUE
No. Maybe. Probably tomorrow. Barring any bedpan adventures.

DOUG
Well, by an odd coincidence, I may be here, too.

SUE
Just working the beach.

DOUG
Would that be a problem?

SUE
Totally not. I'll bring extra salmon.

They shake hands awkwardly.

SUE
Until...then, then.

DOUG
Do me a favour.

SUE
Anything. Well, most things.

DOUG
As you're leaving, don't look back.

SUE
You're as nuts as I am.

DOUG
Time will tell.

SUE
Okay. No looking back.

She sighs.

SUE
Goodbye, Doug.

DOUG
Bye.

She passes him and moves L. He watches her. She EXITS. He turns and looks R at the sea. After a moment, gives a big 'I'm warning you' gesture at whatever he sees there. EXITS R, watching the sea.

From R comes the SOUND of a SEAL CALLING...then it fades.

BLACKOUT
END

Just Add Actors

Andrew Wetmore

Acknowledgements

A great many playwrights and actors heard or took part in early versions of these plays and provided supportive and useful feedback. It really helps to hear and see actors try to work with your script: the glitches, assumptions, and omissions become painfully evident and give you lots to work on in the second draft. Playwrights' Platform in Boston and Merrimack Valley Playwrights in Lowell, Massachusetts; and the writers' group that meets in Annapolis Royal, Nova Scotia, have been both patient and helpful with my fledgling scripts.

Thank you to Brenda Thompson for bringing Moose House Publications into being, providing a way for rural Nova Scotian writers of all sorts of books to get their works into publication.

Andrew Wetmore

About the author

Andrew Wetmore trained as a performer, but concluded relatively early that his skills did not match his enthusiasm in a way that would support a professional acting career. Instead, he has spent decades working with community theatres and regional playwrights. He was the founding chairperson of Dramatists' Co-op, an initiative by the Writers' Federation of Nova Scotia to improve the quality and increase the visibility of Nova-Scotia-written scripts.  For many years he was artistic director of Moveable Feast Theatre, which performed in Quebec and Massachusetts. He founded and coordinated MVP (Merrimack Valley Playwrights), where writers in northern Massachusetts could hear their scripts read by trained actors and get constructive feedback on them from their writing and acting colleagues.

Wetmore was born in Nova Scotia, and returned to the province in 2013 after many years 'down the road.' He is the editor for Moose House Publications, and for the infrastructure team of the Apache Software Foundation.

www.ingramcontent.com/pod-product-compliance
Lightning Source LLC
Chambersburg PA
CBHW071412070526
44578CB00003B/556